Be
Still
AND
Know

GUIDED DEVOTIONAL

Belle City Gifts

A division of
BroadStreet Publishing Group LLC
Savage, Minnesota, USA
Broadstreetpublishing.com

Be Still and Know

978-1-4245-5998-5

Devotional entries composed by Janelle Anthony Breckell, Diane Dahlen, Claire Flores, Shannon Lindsay, and Michelle Winger.

Design by Chris Garborg | www.garborgdesign.com
Edited and compiled by Michelle Winger | www.literallyprecise.com

Printed in China.

20 21 22 22 23   5 4 3 2 1

Something New

"I am about to do something new.
See, I have already begun! Do you not see it?
I will make a pathway through the wilderness.
I will create rivers in the dry wasteland"

ISAIAH 43:19 NLT

Whether you have generated a color-coded list of goals, dreams, and an execution plan for the next 365 days or you've banned resolutions and vowed to make this just another day on the calendar, the clean slate represented by the first day of a new year is filled with an undeniable air of expectation. The excitement of a new bauble or gadget pales in comparison to the promise of a new beginning. Deep down inside, there is a part of us which thinks, "This could be my year!"

Guess what? It *is* your year. This day, and every one that follows, is yours. It is yours to choose who and how to love, to serve, and even to be. And the choice you made in reading this page represents the choice to take this journey in the company of your heavenly Father. That is a beautiful place to start.

Heavenly Father, I give you this year. I ask that you would help me keep you in the forefront of my mind as I make decisions and plans. I want to seek your advice in everything I set my hand to.

DAY 2

All Things New

He who sat on the throne said, "Behold,
I make all things new." And He said to me,
"Write, for these words are true and faithful."
REVELATION 21:5 NKJV

The most beautiful thing about the God we've entrusted our lives to is that he makes all things new. That is a faithful statement—it has always been true and will always be true.

As we begin a new year, empty and full of both bright promise and worrisome unknown, we can rest our souls in the truth that our God will make everything new. Our regrets, mistakes, and failures are nothing compared to his covenanted promise of redemption and newness.

Thank you, Jesus, that you make all things new.
Thank you that your Word is faithful and true,
and I don't have to doubt your promises.
Bring newness to my life this year. Take my regrets
and turn them into new beginnings.

Invisible

The LORD looks down from heaven
and sees the whole human race.
From his throne he observes
all who live on the earth.

PSALM 33:13-14 NLT

Are you feeling invisible today? You may be surrounded by a crowd of
people and yet feel alone and isolated. This may be how the woman who
needed a healing touch from Jesus felt, but was convinced he would never
notice her among so many. She reached out and touched him, and found
him fully aware. Hagar, Sarah's servant, was driven from her home by her
angry mistress. Wandering lost and alone in the wilderness, God saw her
and became her deliverer.

It's difficult to comprehend that as small and insignificant as we are in time
and space, God sees each of us and even knows our name. Others may not
seem to notice or understand, but God knows our whole story. He is always
present, all-seeing, all-wise. No matter where we are, God sees.

*I am so thankful, Lord, that you not only see me physically, but you
see into my heart and mind and know my every thought. Help me
always to remember that I am never invisible to you.*

DAY 4

Patience Now

Be completely humble and gentle;
be patient, bearing with one another in love.
EPHESIANS 4:2 NIV

It has been said that a prayer for patience is a dangerous one because in order to develop it, trials need to come. Patience is developed with much practice; even the simple act of waiting—for anything really—is good practice. Think of the patience Jesus has with us. Before we knew Christ, he waited patiently for us to come to repentance. When we fail to trust him and worry and complain about our circumstances, he waits until we're ready to turn to him once again. He puts up with our foibles and inconsistencies and loves us anyway.

Are you being called to a new level of patience these days? Are you bristling with frustration and anger at things that aren't going your way? Are spiritual growing pains about to wear you out? Then it's time to kneel once again at the throne of grace and ask for help in your time of need.

Oh Lord, forgive me for my impatience today. I am going to pray a bold prayer and ask that you would develop the quality of patience in my life. Help me to cooperate with the process.

My Identity

Once you had no identity as a people;
now you are God's people.
Once you received no mercy;
now you have received God's mercy.

1 PETER 2:10 NLT

There is an emphasis in society on the importance of "finding ourselves."
It seems a valid endeavor. We need to know our gifts and skills and have
an outlet for them: a purpose for living. We need an identity. As Christians,
we have one! First Peter says we are living stones in God's spiritual temple,
royal priests, a chosen people, God's very own possession. Before Christ,
we were without identity and purpose.

Have you lost your identity somewhere along the way? Maybe you've lost
your footing as you've dealt with daily responsibilities? Reaffirm who and
whose you are. You are one who belongs to Christ, called out of darkness to
shine Christ's light in this world!

*God, I want to reaffirm that I am your child. I am forgiven, I have a
new name, and I am part of your kingdom. You have called me out of
darkness to show others your goodness. My identity is in you!*

DAY 6

Not Our Own

I know, LORD, that our lives are not our own.
We are not able to plan our own course.
So correct me, LORD, but please be gentle.
Do not correct me in anger, for I would die.

JEREMIAH 10:23-24 NLT

Jeremiah, a prophet of God, was called to reveal the sins of the Israelites and warn them of coming judgment. His pleas were ignored and the consequences fell when the Babylonians destroyed Jerusalem. Prior to that catastrophe, Jeremiah made one of the most profound statements in the Scriptures. The Israelites insisted on following the lead of the idolatrous nations around them doing things their own way. They seemingly forgot they were God's chosen people and that God had lovingly directed their steps. In their independence, they fell into sin and lost the promised presence of God.

I wonder how many times we forget whose we are and begin to think we can plan our own course in life. Perhaps we are not happy with God's direction and are resisting the road he has asked us to walk. Maybe today you need to pray with Jeremiah:

Correct me, Lord, but please be gentle. Do not correct me in anger, for I would die. I repent of my independence and once again surrender to your direction.

DAY 7

Smelling Good

Now he uses us to spread the knowledge of Christ everywhere,
like a sweet perfume. Our lives are a Christ-like fragrance rising up to God.

2 CORINTHIANS 2:14-15 NLT

What are your favorite fragrances? Freshly baked bread, honeysuckles, lilacs, brewing coffee, or crisp fall air? An aroma can catapult you back in years to a childhood memory or cause an emotion or mood to suddenly arise within you as it links you to a past experience. A woman wearing a lovely perfume shares the fragrance as it permeates the space around her, wafting gently through the air.

Christ wants us to live our lives so that no matter our location, we are disseminating the sweet-smelling perfume of the gospel which then rises up to glorify God. Our gentle, quiet spirits, the peace and joy we exhibit, the kindness, love, and patience we show to others will cause people to turn their heads and say, "What smells so good? I want some of that!"

Oh Jesus, help me to live my life exhibiting your character in everything I do and say. I want to smell good so that my life draw others to you.

Taming the Untamable

Set a guard, O LORD, over my mouth;
keep watch over the door of my lips.

PSALM 141:3 NIV

What a challenge it is for women to master their tongues! Has yours been
out of control lately? It is said that women use an average of 20,000 words
a day, while men only speak 7,000. With that many words pouring out of
our mouths every day, there is simply a greater possibility that some of
them will be hurtful, unkind, and harmful.

What's to be done with our tongues? James describes them as a fire
that is untamable by man. One moment it praises God; the next it curses
man. What a dilemma! It's so wonderful to know that just like the other
challenges we face, we can run to God for a solution. He does what
we cannot do, but we must do our part. Meditate on the Word so that
Scripture flows easily and our consciences are tender. Determine to speak
more about God and less about others. And finally, pray with the psalmist:

Set a guard over my mouth; keep watch over the door of my lips.
Help me, Lord, to speak words of life to those around me.
Help me to swallow words that harm and speak
only words that uplift.

Faith Matters

He (Abraham) was fully convinced that God is able to do whatever he promises. And because of Abraham's faith, God counted him as righteous.

ROMANS 4:21-22 NLT

Sometimes we are hesitant to admit that we are discouraged because our prayers are not being answered. So many godly men and women have believed God for a miracle and not received it on earth. Does that mean their faith was in vain?

God promised Abraham that he would be the father of many nations and that through him all the peoples of the earth would be blessed. He believed even though in the natural it was an impossibility. God saw his faith and counted him as righteous. Hebrews 11 lists other giants of the faith—Abel, Enoch, Noah, Jacob, Joseph, and Moses—and says, "All these people died still believing what God had promised them. They did not receive what was promised, but they saw it all from a distance and welcomed it" (Hebrews 11:13 NLT). There may be prayers we utter that we will not see answered in our lifetime. Can we emulate the saints of old and believe no matter the outcome?

Lord, help me to persevere in faith because my faith alone counts!
You hear my prayers and even if I cannot see your response,
I know you are working!

The Fear Factor

When I am afraid, I will put my trust in you.
I praise God for what he has promised.
I trust in God, so why should I be afraid?

PSALM 56:3-4 NLT

You will notice David did not hesitate to admit when he was afraid! King Saul was pursuing him and so great was his terror that he ran to the enemy's camp—an unlikely place to find refuge. It was bold and risky, but perhaps King Achish would not recognize him, or might consider him a deserter and an asset. Unfortunately, David was found out, reported to the king, and, motivated by more fear, acted like a mad man and was sent away. Fear causes us to do things we normally would not.

It wasn't long before David readjusted his thinking and put his trust once again in God. It is interesting that he says, "*When* I am afraid," not "*If* I am afraid." Fear is a human response and unless counteracted by trust, is at best destructive. What are you afraid of today? Are you magnifying a concern into an impossible mountain of what ifs? Trust Jesus. Remember his promises to you. No matter the outcome, he is in charge!

Lord, I am afraid today, but like David I am going to trust you! I don't have to worry about anything because I know that whatever you allow in my life is designed for my good. I rest in that knowledge.

Remember

I recall all you have done, O LORD;
I remember your wonderful deeds of long ago.
They are constantly in my thoughts.
I cannot stop thinking about your mighty works.

PSALM 77:11-12 NLT

You've heard of "selective memory," when a person remembers only the bits of the past that are convenient while forgetting those that are not. Maybe that's why the "good ol' days" seem so good! All through Scripture, we are commanded to remember. Think about how many times Moses admonished the Israelites to recall all that the Lord had done for them through the years. To remember how they had provoked God and suffered the consequences, so they wouldn't repeat the same mistakes.

Remembering what God has done builds our faith. Each time he proves himself faithful to you, another brick in your foundation of trust is laid. The precedent has been set and whenever he moves on your behalf, the bedrock of your faith grows stronger. You know that he brought you through before and he will do it again. Take time today to remember and to thank God for all he has done.

Forgive me, Lord, for forgetting the way you have worked in my life.
I am prone to fret as though this time you won't come through!
Thank you for your faithfulness to me and for all you have done!

Sitting With Sinners

"Go and learn what this means,
'I desire mercy, not sacrifice.' For I have come
to call not the righteous but sinners."

MATTHEW 9:13 NRSV

Have you ever felt like you haven't been getting recognition for all the work you have done, either in your job or at home? Have there been times when you have seen other people acknowledged for doing seemingly little? Hard work without appreciation can seem very unfair.

Imagine then how those Pharisees felt when Jesus chose to sit with the sinners! They were bothered by the fact that Jesus was spending time with the unrighteous when they had devoted their whole lives to obeying and working under the law. Jesus responded by saying we don't earn forgiveness; rather, we receive it as a gift. We are all sinners, and yet Jesus chooses to sit with us because he wants to show us mercy. Sit with him and freely receive it!

Lord Jesus, I know that I am a sinner before you, and yet I thank you that you have chosen to sit with me here and now, offering your grace and mercy. I receive your forgiveness as a gift, knowing that it is not what I do that makes you accept me. Help me to be merciful to others, as you have been to me.

Give and Get

A generous person will prosper;
whoever refreshes others will be refreshed.

PROVERBS 11:25 NIV

You get what you give. It's a simple principle, and one that the Bible endorses. We are not like a takeaway cup that becomes useless once it has been emptied. In God's upside-down kingdom, the more we empty ourselves, the more we are filled back up! It can be hard to let go of money, or time, or energy for the sake of others. However, if we understand that God is using us to give to others, we can also trust that he will find a way to provide for us. And he does!

Is your tank on empty, needing to be filled up? Do you need refreshing? Be generous and willing to encourage someone in need; there are plenty of people around you if you make yourself aware. As you give, the Lord will return to you.

Dear Lord, show me the people in my life that need my generosity. Show me those who need my time, my prayers, and my encouragement. As I give to others, please fill me up and restore my soul so that I can live a life that is full of you.

Faith Please

Without faith it is impossible to please God, for whoever would approach
him must believe that he exists and that he rewards those who seek him.

HEBREWS 11:6 NRSV

We spend a lot of our lives trying to please people, whether it is a tidy
house, a delicious meal, a great birthday present, or new clothes. It seems
that to gain approval we need to do things that make us look
good to others.

This is often how we approach God, with great effort to do the right things
to please him. But the Bible says that it is impossible to please him without
faith. What is faith? It is a belief in your heart and a confession with your
mouth that Jesus Christ is Lord. It is not what you do that will please God; it
is a heart that seeks to follow him. Approach the Lord today with a surety
that he is pleased with you, not because of what you *do* but because of
what you believe.

*Father, I come with a heart that wants to please you. Forgive me for
thinking that all the good things that I do are more important than a
heart that believes in you and continually seeks your w ill. I have faith
in you, and I will wait patiently for the reward of seeking you.*

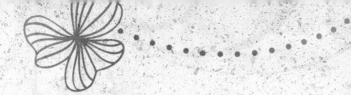

Born of God

As many as received Him, to them He gave the right to become children of God, to those who believe in His name: who were born, not of blood, nor of the will of the flesh, nor of the will of man, but of God.

JOHN 1:12-13 NKJV

When children are born, the most significant part in shaping their identity is knowing to whom they are born. They will also continue to be molded by where they are born and who they have to nurture them as they grow. We all have different stories regarding this. We have birth parents, and the circumstance of our conception can be labeled anything from desired to unwanted.

You may have been nurtured by loving parents, uncaring parents, struggling parents, or perhaps even no parents. However, those of us who believe in God have something in common. We are all children of God. It was God who created us and brought us into the world. It is God who has been watching over us since we took our first breath. It was God who was overjoyed when we accepted him as our Savior. We have been born again into God's family and nothing in this earth can take that away from us.

Heavenly Father, thank you that you have called me into your family. Thank you that you love and care for me as your precious child.

Hear Me

Hear me when I call, O God of my righteousness!
You have relieved me in my distress;
Have mercy on me, and hear my prayer.

PSALM 4:1 NKJV

Who do you call when you are feeling upset and stressed? Is there someone in your life who will listen to you in your time of need? Are you confident that God is always near and you can call on him when you are distressed?

The Lord knows your heart and what you are facing; he alone is able to relieve you of your burden. He is a God of mercy, which means that it doesn't matter what you have done, or how big a battle you face, his loving-kindness is able to save you in your time of need. He will hear you, so call out to him.

Dear Lord, I call out to you now, believing in your goodness and ability to ease my burdens. I know that you hear me as I pray. Thank you for listening to me. Hear my heart when I can't express it in words. Lift me up and give me peace.

Rejoice Always

Rejoice always, pray continually, give thanks in
all circumstances; for this is God's will for you
in Christ Jesus.

1 THESSALONIANS 5:16-18 NIV

Life doesn't always work out the way we want it to. The circumstances that
we find ourselves in can leave us feeling disappointed and even resentful.
We have expected God's goodness without realizing that part of the
Christian walk involves suffering.

It is not that God wants you to go through hardship, but he wants you
to experience his joy and presence at all times. This is why we are to give
thanks in all our circumstances, whether joyous or painful. He is ab
le to lift you up, to allow you to feel joy, and to bring you closer to him.
Rejoice always!

*Dear Lord, help me to come to you in the hard times as well as the
easy times. Thank you that you are a good God who cares about me.
Thank you that I can trust you with my life. Thank you that
you are present in all of my circumstances. Remind me to
rejoice in you, always.*

Courage for Christ

It is my eager expectation and hope that I will not be at all ashamed, but that with full courage now as always Christ will be honored in my body, whether by life or by death.

PHILIPPIANS 1:20 ESV

What are your hopes for your life? Perhaps you want a meaningful career, to go on worldwide adventures, to become a wife, or to simply raise wise and wonderful children. Of course we all hope to live a life that honors God, but are we courageous about our faith as much as Paul expresses in this verse?

Paul knew that the Christ that he preached was offensive to many people; the gospel was very hard for others to accept. However, Paul was confident that eventually all would know the truth of Christ, and in this, he knew that he would not be ashamed. Would you allow this to be your hope as well? Honor God with your whole life by being courageous enough to share Christ with the world.

Jesus, I want to serve and honor you with my whole life. Teach me to understand the gospel and then give me the courage to share you with others around me. Let me hope and expect, as Paul did, that I will not be at all ashamed.

Yes to Grace

The grace of God has appeared that offers salvation to all people.
It teaches us to say "No" to ungodliness and worldly passions,
and to live self-controlled, upright and godly lives in this present age.
TITUS 2:11-12 NIV

When you hear a word often enough it begins to lose its impact. This can
happen when we see words like *grace* and *forgiveness*; they surround us
because they are core to our Christian faith. Instead of switching off when
you read or hear the word *grace*, remember that grace is actually equivalent
to Jesus.

Jesus defeated the power of sin in our lives and we no longer have to earn
our salvation through good works! Grace is powerful because it gets to the
heart of the matter. You are no longer judged because of your outward sin.
The Father can see your heart of repentance and you will be forgiven. His
forgiveness transforms our hearts, and this is what gives us the strength to
say no to ungodliness and live righteously. Say yes to his grace today!

*Jesus, thank you for sacrificing your life on the cross,
so that I can experience salvation. I need the power of your grace
working in my life so I can resist worldly passions. Forgive my sin
and transform my heart, so I can live a godly life in this moment.*

Unshakable

Since we are receiving a kingdom that cannot be shaken, let us be thankful,
and so worship God acceptably with reverence and awe.

HEBREWS 12:28 NIV

It is probably easier to understand the power of kingdoms back in the
day when monarchy reigned supreme. These days, it might be easier to
recognize power and authority in our politics, world leaders, and law. As we
well know, not many political systems, leaders, or even societal law stand
the test of time. Leaders are replaced, a new governance structure is set
up, and laws change as society does.

We live in a very unsettled world! It's little wonder that a good majority of
us are anxious about the future. This doesn't need to be our outlook. The
Bible says that we are receiving a kingdom that cannot be shaken! This
means that our God will reign with justice, mercy, and peace. You can be
thankful because you have a bright future ahead of you. The good news is
that he has already begun his work. We can worship him as our King,
even today.

*Dear Lord, I revere you as the sovereign Lord of this world and also of
my heart. I worship you because you are awesome. You will one day
bring your magnificent plans to completion. Help me to live with the
hope of your kingdom that cannot be shaken.*

Crown of Life

Blessed is the man who remains steadfast under trial, for when he has stood the test he will receive the crown of life, which God has promised to those who love him.

JAMES 1:12 ESV

"When will these hard times ever end, Lord?" Do you find yourself praying again and again to be relieved of the challenges of life? You might be struggling through grief, engaged in conflict with someone, giving up an addiction, or just trying to make it through each day without collapsing from exhaustion. Life presents a lot of testing and temptation.

God doesn't promise an easy life. He does, however, promise a great reward to those who will endure the trials. Strength doesn't have to look like you have it all together when things are hard. It doesn't mean that you come out unscathed in your battles. It means that you have been patient through the struggle and that you have continued to love and trust God. The crown of life is your future hope. One day you will receive God's eternal kingdom, and your troubles will have been worth standing through. Remain steadfast; your reward is coming.

Lord, teach me to have patience through these times that seem almost too hard to endure. Forgive me for wanting to escape the challenge and look for an easier way out. Remind me of the value of resisting tmptation and standing strong. I look forward to receiving the crown of eternal life.

Name Above All

I bow down toward your holy temple
and give thanks to your name
for your steadfast love and your faithfulness;
for you have exalted your name
and your word above everything.

PSALM 138:2 NRSV

What have you been looking toward in your life lately? Is any one thing taking priority over everything else? In Bible times, people built statues and placed them in high places to worship them. It was their way of looking to something that they could put their trust in: something they could ask for help or favor from. These days we don't have statues, but we have food, entertainment, relationships, careers, celebrities, and money to idolize.

In a world where so many things are competing for our worship, it is good to remember the God whose name is higher than any other thing. He is worthy to be worshiped because of his faithfulness and everlasting love toward us. To bow down to God's holy temple was to approach the place where God dwelled. Since Christ has now redeemed us, we have become the place where God's Spirit dwells. Are you able to give thanks to him in your heart, and let him take his rightful place again in your life?

Lord God, I want to thank you for your love and faithfulness in my life. I want to serve you and worship you above every other thing on earth. Help me to show you love by remaining faithful to you.

Clothed in Grace

You were taught, with regard to your former way of life,
to put off your old self, which is being corrupted by its deceitful desires;
to be made new in the attitude of your minds.

EPHESIANS 4:22-23 NIV

Fashion comes and goes with every new season. If you don't follow it closely, you could be wearing last year's wardrobe before you realize that you are totally out of date! You may not care much about fashion, but living in the past can indicate a lack of acceptance of the present.

Such is the illustration with our salvation. When we accepted Christ as our Savior, we accepted a new life—one that is free from the power of sin, and one that began our spiritual, eternal life. If you feel like you have been caught wearing sin like an ugly, old garment, take it off! Instead, clothe yourself with an attitude of forgiveness and the freedom that was given to you through Jesus.

Jesus, forgive me for going back to some of my old sinful habits. Thank you that you have given me a new life that allows me to have freedom from my sinful nature. Give me an attitude that willingly throws off my old life, so I can live by your grace.

Held in His Hand

You, God, see the trouble of the afflicted;
you consider their grief and take it in hand.
The victims commit themselves to you;
you are the helper of the fatherless.

PSALM 10:14 NIV

The problems of life are seen all around us, sometimes on a daily basis. We see troubled families, poverty, and sickness. Maybe you are experiencing some of these afflictions. It is comforting to know that God sees our troubles. He is not a God that stands at a distance. He takes our grief in his hand.

You may feel helpless, but God is the helper. When the victims of loneliness, abuse, hunger, and poverty seek out God, he will meet them. God carefully watches over the hurting and he offers his hand. Jesus knew what it was like to suffer. He experienced trouble and grief, so we know he understands. Will you trust him to intervene when you are feeling troubled? Will you commit yourself to him, so that he can help you? He cares for humanity, and he cares for you!

Heavenly Father, I bring my troubled heart before you today. I ask you to consider my situation. I give it over to you, knowing that you understand and that you care for me. Help me trust you as a good Father who is always there to help me in my time of need.

No Longer Captive

You did not receive the spirit of bondage again to fear, but you received the Spirit of adoption by whom we cry out, "Abba, Father."

ROMANS 8:15 NKJV

When a slave is released from captivity it is often hard for them to know what to do with their freedom. In fact, many slaves, in Biblical times, would choose to remain servants (bondservants) to their masters, not knowing how to *belong* elsewhere. We probably don't relate to slavery the way the Israelites did, but we can understand feeling powerless over sin, emotions, or even in relationships.

When Jesus defeated death on the cross, he introduced a way for us to be free from our former lives of captivity to sin and death. We no longer have to fear that old life; we have a new life that is living by the Spirit. We are children of God. When we truly understand our freedom, we can begin to let go of the areas of our lives that hold us back.

Abba Father, thank you for freeing me from the power of sin and darkness. Thank you that I now belong to your family and I can live protected in your love. Help me to recognize the areas in my life that keep me from living in this freedom, and give me the strength to let them go.

Call Me

Call to me and I will answer you,
and I will tell you great and mighty things,
which you do not know.

JEREMIAH 33:3 NASB

Have you ever used caller ID to make sure that you don't answer phone calls that you don't want to? Maybe you haven't, but we all know the feeling of not wanting to talk to someone. Maybe we're concerned about being uncomfortable, we don't know what to say, or we just don't want to have to say "no" to whatever is asked of us.

Let's not make that same assumption about God's response when he hears us call out to him! God himself asks us to call on him, and he tells us that he will answer. God knows us—heart, mind, and soul. He is never going to be stuck without a response. He desires communication with us. He wants us to know so much about him that we begin to understand great and mighty things that we didn't know before. Give him a call today!

Hello, Lord Jesus. Thank you that you want to listen to me. I have a lot of things to talk to you about. I would love some answers, too. Would you reveal something of yourself to me today? I know that there are many great and wonderful things that I don't know yet, and I am ready to listen.

Rules of Happiness

Happy are those whom you discipline, O LORD,
and whom you teach out of your law.

PSALM 94:12 NRSV

Discipline is often followed by tears, so it seems surprising when the Bible associates discipline with happiness! While we may feel ashamed when the Lord convicts our heart of wrongdoing, we need to recognize that God's correction is ultimately for our good. He wants us to do what is right because he loves us.

It is said that creating boundaries for children gives them contentment because they are clear about right and wrong. This is the way that God teaches us from his law. He doesn't want to enforce rules so that he can punish us when we fail; he wants us to know righteousness so that we can freely walk in it. Will you let him correct, guide, and instruct you in the way you should go? Be blessed as he continues a good work in you.

Lord, thank you for guiding me into every good thing. Give me ears to hear and eyes to see the truth of your ways. Help me to learn from your instruction and to know your grace when I need correction. Let me experience the joy of your discipline.

Hateful or Grateful

Do everything without grumbling or arguing, so that you may become blameless and pure, children of God without fault in a warped and crooked generation. Then you will shine among them like stars in the sky.

PHILIPPIANS 2:14-15 NIV

Most companies have a department dedicated to dealing with complaints. It is an apt indication of our human nature: we complain when our "rights" have not been met. The problem with complaining is that it focuses our attitude on wrongdoing.

What a different world it would be if we could first look at our own hearts and admit our wrongdoing before pointing the finger at others. This kind of humility is rare and precious. It can only really be achieved by allowing God's grace to permeate your life. It is Jesus that makes you blameless and pure, and if you can imitate his humility, your life will shine like a bright star amidst the darkness.

Jesus, I acknowledge that my immediate reaction is to complain and argue to show others their faults. Remind me to search my own heart and to be humble in my approach to others. Thank you for your ultimate example of humility. Let me experience the full measure of your grace that I may follow your example.

At the Crossroads

This is what the LORD says:
"Stop at the crossroads and look around.
Ask for the old, godly way, and walk in it.
Travel its path, and you will find rest for your souls."
But you reply, "No, that's not the road we want!"

JEREMIAH 6:16 NLT

Sometimes our journey of life stops us in our tracks and requires us to make a decision about which way to go. Some of us continue on the path we were headed, others run quickly in another direction, while still others take so long to decide that it seems they are forever standing at the same crossroad!

God gave the people of Israel some clear directions on how to steer away from their inevitable path of destruction. First, we need to stop and evaluate our past and future situation. Second, we ask for the godly way, and then we walk in it. We can find the way through what has been written in Scripture. The Bible tells us a lot about who God is and how he wants his children to conduct their lives. Don't be stubborn like the Israelites and reply, "No, that's not what I want." Obedience will ultimately bring you peace.

Lord, give me wisdom to choose the godly path that you have set before me. Help me to take time to stop and listen to your guidance. Allow me to rely on your strength to say yes to the right way.

Beautiful Layers

For this very reason, make every effort to add to your faith goodness;
and to goodness, knowledge; and to knowledge, self-control; and to self-
control, perseverance; and to perseverance, godliness; and to godliness,
mutual affection; and to mutual affection, love.

2 PETER 1:5-7 NIV

The art of a painting lies not in what you see, but in the process that has gone
into making it what it has become. Usually a painting begins with inspiration: an
idea or emotion that wants to be expressed. It proceeds with sketching, color,
texture, and variations in between. A painter rarely produces exactly what they
originally pictured.

Our life with God can be like a painting. It begins with our faith. Our belief
in Jesus sets up our canvas, but the Scriptures call us to add to the depth of
our faith by applying colors of goodness, knowledge, and self-control. The
beauty emerges as we add perseverance, godliness, affection, and love.
These things take time to develop in us. They can involve mistakes, and
they can make us look very different. Do you need to add anything to your
faith today? Will you make the extra effort to become beautiful by applying
goodness, perseverance, or love to your life?

*Thank you, Jesus, that you have begun a good work in me. I have
faith in your saving grace. Today, Lord, I need to add some spiritual
discipline to my faith. Help me to know you more, help me to control
my emotions, help me to persevere, and help me to love.*

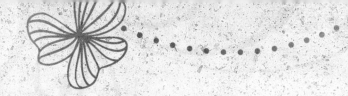

Summer and Winter

The day is yours, and yours also the night;
you established the sun and moon.
It was you who set all the boundaries of the earth;
you made both summer and winter.

PSALM 74:16-17 NIV

Those who live in a cold climate understand that winters can get long. As the amount of daylight decreases, it's easy to find discouragement or depression creeping in. Sometimes this is a direct result of just needing more vitamin D to compensate for the lack of sunlight. But sometimes the Lord allows this to drive you to a place of finding a deeper degree of contentment in him.

God created the seasons. They are his making. Winter treasures are like manna—the same manna would be rotten in the summer. Manna that is provided on a daily basis refreshes us and provides the kind of nourishment we need.

God, help me to make the most out of this season. I don't want to live in complaint or wish away the winter. There are treasures to be found in this place that I don't want to miss.

Built Up

Encourage one another and build one another up,
just as you are doing.
1 THESSALONIANS 5:11 ESV

The church was meant to be a place of unity—that is why it is described as the *body* of Christ. In order to function well, the body needs every part to be connected and working well together. When there is disunity or factions, the church suffers as a sick person, unable to operate in a healthy way.

It is very important, then, that you belong to a healthy community of believers. It is even more important that you consider yourself a vital part of your church and that you recognize the need to encourage others within so you can help strengthen the family of God. Again, as healthy muscles are built up and become stronger, so does a church that loves and encourages one another. Do you need to find a church that is encouraging? Do you need to be the one who encourages your body of believers today? Surround yourself with encouraging believers and watch your strength increase.

*Lord God, thank you for putting good Christian people in my life.
I pray that I would find a way to encourage these people so that
we can become strong together. Allow me to be uplifted
as I encourage others.*

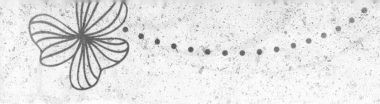

Approved

Go, eat your bread with joy,
and drink your wine with a merry heart,
for God has already approved what you do.

ECCLESIASTES 9:7 ESV

All children want to know that their parents are proud of them. It's an innate human need—to be affirmed in our capabilities and to be praised for our work. But every good parent will tell you the same thing: they are proud of their children no matter what. Children earn adoration simply by belonging to the parents.

Do you believe that your heavenly Father is pleased with you? Do you walk in peace knowing that you have his approval? Beloved, remember that when you are in Christ, his blood covers all your wrongdoing. You don't have to wonder if God is pleased with you; your identity through his Son is enough to warrant his full blessing, his true approval, and his fierce love.

Father, I am so humbled by the work that Christ did on the cross for me. I am humbled by the place I hold in your family. Help me to remember that you are pleased with me. I know that there is nowhere I can go where I won't be covered in your love. I want to live a life worthy of being called yours.

Been with Jesus

The leaders saw that Peter and John were not afraid to speak, and they understood that these men had no special training or education. So they were amazed. Then they realized that Peter and John had been with Jesus.

ACTS 4:13 NCV

Christians want to be like Jesus. We ask him daily for his grace, mercy, humility, and love. But the surest way to be like someone is to spend time in their presence.

Have you been with Jesus enough that people take notice? When someone is with you, do they see the attitudes and evidence of Christ in you? By spending time soaking in the presence of the Lord, reading his Word, and learning his ways, people will soon realize that you've been with him. You will be marked as one who has been in his presence and your life will show his glory to those around you.

God, help me to long for your presence so much that I cannot go without you. Help me to need your Word the same way I need food. Give me a consistent longing to be with you so that when people see me, they will see the clear mark of Christ.

The Watching World

How great is the goodness
you have stored up for those who fear you.
You lavish it on those who come to you for protection,
blessing them before the watching world.

PSALM 31:19 NLT

Have you ever looked at someone and noticed that the blessing of God is on their life in a remarkable way? Maybe they've received a clear miracle, or they have been inexplicably successful in their endeavors. Maybe they have an unearthly joy that flows out contagiously. No matter what the evidence is, you know without a doubt that the hand of God is on them.

Many times when we first come to God, we come for protection—seeking salvation and security—and he gives us those things, but he doesn't stop there. He also gives us his goodness, his kindness, his love. And once we begin to receive the goodness of such a great God, the world takes notice.

Thank you, God, that you lavish your goodness on me.
I came to you out of gratitude for what your Son did for me.
I came to you for protection from death and for eternal life.
But you gave me so much more than that. You gave me your
goodness. You gave me your blessings. Let the world take notice;
and let them glorify you because of it.

Choose Joy

Always be joyful. Pray continually, and give thanks whatever happens.
That is what God wants for you in Christ Jesus.
1 THESSALONIANS 5:16-18 NCV

We all want to be happy. We spend our lives chasing the idea of happiness only to find it just out of our reach. But when we stop chasing happiness, and start choosing joy—that is when we truly begin to live out our lives to the fullest.

Happiness comes by chance; joy is a choice. Joy is choosing to be thankful when we could be ungrateful. It's choosing to see the good when we could see the bad. It's constant prayer coupled with continual thanksgiving because when we choose joy in our hearts, nothing—not even the worst of circumstances—can rob it from us.

Thank you, God for the blessings you've given me. Thank you that while I have little control over my circumstances, I do have total control over whether or not I am joyful in my own life. Help me to build an attitude of joy and to practice a heart of thankfulness so that I can live the life that you want me to live in your Son.

Illuminated

"All who do evil hate the light and do not come to the light,
so that their deeds may not be exposed. But those who do
what is true come to the light, so that it may be clearly seen that
their deeds have been done in God."

JOHN 3:20-21 NRSV

From the beginning of time, humans have known to be ashamed when they have done wrong. Look at Adam and Eve who hid once they were aware of their great sin against God. However, God is light; he is able to expose everything that is hidden. This can explain why we don't like to communicate with God when we know that we have done wrong—we don't want our deeds exposed.

But Jesus changed all of that. The Bible says that those who believe in him are not condemned! We have come to the light and believed in Jesus; we have received the truth and are saved. If you are struggling with sin, remember that those deeds can be forgiven because you are in God.

Heavenly Father, sometimes I feel burdened because of my sin and I want to hide from you. I ask you to relieve me of this burden, and remind me that I am forgiven. Let me approach you with boldness, exposing all of my sin, accepting your grace, so that I can walk confidently in your light.

DAY 38

Softly Spoken

A soft answer turns away wrath,
But a harsh word stirs up anger.
PROVERBS 15:1 NKJV

Have you ever marveled at how you can maneuver your entire car, often with just one hand? (Not that we would admit this, of course!) It is typically very small parts that control an entire machine. The Bible says that this is the way our tongue works. Have you noticed how easy it is to control an environment not only with what you say, but the volume and tone of your words?

Are you guilty of reacting harshly when someone speaks angrily or unfairly to you? Don't worry, we all are. The problem with a harshly returned word is that it stirs up more anger and this becomes a cycle that is hard to break. Are you able to allow God to remind you in these situations that returning anger with softness will help the situation? Rely on the Holy Spirit to give you gentle and wise words and see how God can bring peace to your difficult situations.

Holy Spirit, guide me in my conversations and even confrontations with others. I am sorry when I have reacted harshly and said the wrong things to people around me. Give me soft words and a gentle heart.

Faithful with the Few

"His master replied, 'Well done, good and faithful servant! You have been faithful with a few things; I will put you in charge of many things. Come and share your master's happiness!'"

MATTHEW 25:21 NIV

It is easy to be discontented with our lives. We think we should be doing more with our education, children, careers, or other responsibilities. We look at others' successes and wonder why we don't seem to have achieved as much. We keep waiting for the day our boss gives us that promotion, or our children achieve great things, or we finally reach that level of income where we can be happy.

When Jesus told the parable of the committed servant that was entrusted with his master's duties, he made a point of focusing on how well the servant did with the *few* things that were put in front of him. What do you have in front of you today, this week, or this year? It may not look like much, but Jesus is asking you to be faithful to him with whatever you have been given. If you are faithful with these few things, God invites you to rejoice with him. It is then that you will see him bring you more.

Heavenly Father, I am sorry for asking for too much, too quickly. Allow me to be diligent and content with the few responsibilities that you have put in front of me right now. Help me to experience your joy and be ready for the greater responsibilities that you may bring.

DAY 40

Hills not Heels

The LORD God is my strength;
He will make my feet like deer's feet,
and He will make me walk on my high hills.

HABAKKUK 3:19 NKJV

Make sure you read that verse right. God isn't going to make you walk in your high heels; that would just be mean! Sure, we like to get dressed up from time to time, but we know that high heels should be left behind when we need to do some real walking!

When you need strength, the Lord God is there to help. Like a deer, we want to be able to walk through the hard times gracefully and climb our mountains with steady feet. We don't want to be overcome with weariness, and we certainly don't want to be stumbling the whole way through our difficulties. Are you in need of God's strength today? Instead of reaching for your heels, remember the high hills and God's grace that is yours to help you walk up them!

Lord God, be my strength today. I have some difficult things to face and I want to be gracious and able to endure the hills. I trust you to guide my each and every step.

Sheep Need a Shepherd

> "I am the good shepherd. The good shepherd
> lays down his life for the sheep."
>
> JOHN 10:11 NRSV

It would be nice to be compared to an animal that is nobler than a sheep! However, seeing ourselves as sheep makes for a good analogy. Sheep are one of those animals that depend on a shepherd to get them through life. Sheep need to be led to food and water, they need shelter provided for them, and they need someone to protect them from harm.

Jesus said that *he* is the good shepherd and it is good to remind ourselves that we absolutely need him. Without Jesus we are lost. Without Jesus we are hungry. Without Jesus we are not safe. Jesus was willing to lay down his life to save you, to guide you, and to protect you. He promises to walk with you, because he is a *good* shepherd. Trust in his goodness today.

Jesus, thank you for laying down your life so that I could be saved. Please guide me today, as you have been guiding me every day. I trust in you to provide for me and to protect me. Help me to know your goodness as I am led by you, my good shepherd.

DAY 42

His Spirit in Us

God has not given us a spirit of fear,
but of power and of love and of a sound mind.

2 TIMOTHY 1:7 NKJV

When we come to Christ, he puts his Spirit inside of us. And the Spirit of the Lord is a Spirit of freedom, of love, of power, and of courage. We can no longer rightly identify ourselves as fearful people. We can't call ourselves timid. We can't act unloving toward others. Because each of those things go directly against the Spirit that is now dwelling within us.

As people of God, we must step forward to live a life that is the visible expression of the invisible God. We have been given full power to love, to be brave, and to think soundly. All we have to do is surrender our own will to God so that his Spirit can move freely in us. Then we will see our own life, as well as the lives of those around us, be transformed.

Thank you, God, for putting your Spirit within me. You have given me your power, your love, and a strong mind to do your will and to bring you glory. Help me to remain sensitive to your Spirit so I can represent you well through my life.

He Is Faithful

All of God's promises have been fulfilled in Christ
with a resounding "Yes!"
2 CORINTHIANS 1:20 NLT

The faithfulness of God is something we so easily find ourselves questioning. Though he has proven himself time and time again throughout history, we still wonder whether or not he will come through for us.

But the reality is that whether the sun is shining or the rain is pouring, whether your song comes easily or your tears pour freely, he continues to be faithful. No matter how long you wait, he remains. He will never turn his back on you, and he will never forget the promises he has made. He sees you. He sees you on the nights when you're weary and ready to give up, but instead you bow your head and bless his name. He sees you when you're at the end of yourself and you cry out to him in desperation. He sees and he understands.

Lord, give me the strength to wait on your promises
and to never lose faith in your faithfulness.

DAY 44

My Bravery

"Have I not commanded you? Be strong and courageous.
Do not be afraid; do not be discouraged, for the LORD your
God will be with you wherever you go."

JOSHUA 1:9 NIV

What does it mean to be commanded to be brave? We often think of bravery as an innate character quality. You're either a bold person, or you're not. And if we are being completely honest, few of us truly feel brave. There is a lot that scares us. We are afraid of failure, of death, of the unknown, and even of insignificance. We don't feel courageous when faced with opposition or hardship, and even those of us who have some resolve to be bold can lose it quickly in the wrong circumstance.

The key to obeying this command is understanding that when we become followers of Jesus Christ, *his* bravery becomes our own. Through his grace and in his power, we are brave. We are able to face the obstacles in our lives with strength and resolve because we have a mighty God who goes before us and behind us.

Lord, remind me continually that I can be strong and courageous because you are with me. I don't have to fear because you have cloaked me with your bravery. When I begin to feel frightened and overwhelmed, remind me of your power and your grace for me.

Growing in Love

As we live in God, our love grows more perfect.
So we will not be afraid on the day of judgment,
but we can face him with confidence because we live
like Jesus here in this world.

1 JOHN 4:17 NLT

Love is hard. It means sacrificing our own priorities for those of another. It goes against our natural flesh instincts. In and of ourselves, love is not our natural reaction or response to the people around us. We have to grow in love and we can only learn this properly from the God who is inherently love.

Without God, we are incapable of truly loving. We can try our hardest to be people who love one another, but sooner or later we will fail at it if we don't have God's heart in us.

Lord God, I want to represent your heart to the world. I know that I am not yet perfect in love. I need you to love others through me. I need to see others through your eyes so I can love them flawlessly as you do. Remove my heart of stone and give me a heart of flesh that beats with your love for this world and everyone in it.

Not Disappointed

You will be rewarded for this;
your hope will not be disappointed.
PROVERBS 23:18 NLT

We've all been disappointed numerous times in our lives. The hard truth is that whenever we hope for something, we put ourselves at risk to be let down. We've all learned this lesson the hard way too many times to not brace ourselves for disappointment in our dreaming.

But there is one hope that will never be lost. No matter how long we find ourselves waiting, or how distant the fulfillment may seem to us—when we put our faith in God, we will not be let down. We will someday clearly see the result of our belief in his coming kingdom. The trust we've placed in his promises will be rewarded, and our hearts will not be disappointed.

Lord Jesus, thank you that you will fulfill my hope in you. I have been disappointed by many people and things in my life, but I know that you won't let me down. Thank you that my heart is safe with you.

DAY 47

I Am Yours

He predestined us for adoption to sonship through Jesus Christ, in accordance with his pleasure and will—to the praise of his glorious grace, which he has freely given us in the One he loves.

EPHESIANS 1:5-6 NIV

No matter what life gives to you, or what it takes from you, one thing is sure. You are a child of God and nothing can change that truth. He paid a high price for your soul. Whether you feel worthy of his love or not, you're wrapped up in it.

He is a good Father. He delights in being kind to you. He inhabits your praise and he enjoys your prayers. There is so much power in understanding your identity as a child of God. As you dwell on the goodness of God today, remember that his heart is for you. There is no good thing in him that has not been extended to you through his Son.

Thank you, God, for being a good Father to me. Thank you that I am one of yours—that I am your child and nothing can change that. Help me not to doubt your love but instead to walk in the power of knowing who I am in you.

Kindness

Instead, be kind to each other, tenderhearted, forgiving one another,
just as God through Christ has forgiven you.

EPHESIANS 4:32 NLT

We must be careful not to judge others quickly based on our limited perception. We mustn't assume things about people based on what we've heard or what little we've observed. The reality is that we truly can't know the full story of those around us. We have no understanding of the losses they've endured or the hardships they've faced. We can never fully know the state of another human heart.

Treating one another with kindness is so important because kindness is always fair. Kindness is appropriate for any person in any circumstance. When we are quick to judge, we are sure to miss the whole picture and act wrongly. But when we are quick in kindness, we will always be acting rightly.

Fill my heart with kindness toward others, Lord. Remove the desire to judge others. Soften my heart and humble me so that I will not be a harsh critic of those whose stories I haven't read. Let me be slow to assumption and quick to love.

Level Ground

Teach me to do your will,
for you are my God;
may your good Spirit
lead me on level ground.

PSALM 143:10 NIV

Walking before God on the path of righteousness can feel like an impossible task. Just when we begin to feel holy, we succumb to temptation and we fall. We are reminded all at once of our innate humanity and overwhelming need for God.

We don't immediately know how to do God's will when we get saved; we have to be taught. We don't naturally begin to walk in his ways; we need to be led. The beautiful thing about salvation is that we aren't expected to do any of it on our own. God puts his Spirit within us and leads us in righteousness on level ground. The sanctified, Christian life is only possible when we completely surrender ourselves to the grace of God, the teaching of Jesus Christ, and the leading of the Holy Spirit.

Thank you, God, that you don't expect me to live a righteous life in my own strength. I need your grace and you give it freely. Thank you for teaching me and guiding me every step of the way, so I can bring you the glory and the honor you are worthy of.

Much Comfort

We share in the many sufferings of Christ. In the same way,
much comfort comes to us through Christ.

2 CORINTHIANS 1:5 NCV

Life is full of beauty and hope and promise. But life also carries with it
ugliness, pain, and disappointment. If you haven't suffered, you haven't
lived. It's just the way of things. You can put on the bravest of faces and
walk straight through the pain, but the reality is that even the strongest
need a place to let down their guard, to cry, to hurt, to feel, and to be
comforted.

Our God isn't lofty or distant from us. He lived life as we do on this earth
and he felt the same pain. There is no better comforter than someone
who has been exactly where you are, enduring the same suffering. Christ is
our comfort. When we have trouble and sorrow, he is our consolation. He
brings us to himself and he holds us; he hears us. Pour your heart out
to him, your joys and your sorrows.

*Lord Jesus, I know that when I run to you in my suffering your
comfort will go further and heal me faster than any other comforter. I
need you to be my safe place. When I am hurting, remind me to run to
you first before I go to anyone or anything else.*

Precious

Because you are precious to me,
because I give you honor and love you,
I will give other people in your place;
I will give other nations to save your life.

ISAIAH 43:4 NCV

Do you know how precious your life is to God? We have all heard a million times about how he loved the world so much that he sent his Son to die for us, but do we truly understand how desperately God longs for us? How passionately he pursues us?

God's love is the most powerful force in the entire universe and it is focused on you. His love can cover any sin that you've committed or ever will commit. He is always ready to bring you back to himself. Never allow shame to keep you from his love. No matter how far you feel you've gone, you are never beyond repair.

Dear Jesus, thank you that your love is not just something you speak about, but it's something you proved when you died for me. You paid the highest price for love and I can never thank you enough. Help me to know how much you truly do love me so that I can take the love I've been shown by you and help others come to know your love that same way.

Water Isn't Concrete

Peter said, "Lord, if it is really you, then command me to come to
you on the water." Jesus said, "Come." And Peter left the boat
and walked on the water to Jesus.

MATTHEW 14:28-29 NCV

Have you ever stepped out in "blind faith" and said yes to something crazy
that God called you to? The valley of decision can be long and difficult, so
when we finally take that step of saying yes, we can expect everything to
come together almost instantly on the other side.

But, when God calls you to get out of the boat, to walk on the water with
him,—you can't expect to step out onto solid ground. Water will never be
concrete. Why are we surprised at the raging waves that at any moment
could sweep us under? The circumstances in life are never going to be sure.
Our plans are never going to go off without a hitch. After all, we're trying to
walk on water. But if we keep our eyes focused on his, we can walk across
even the most tempestuous waters, as if they were simply solid ground.

*Lord, keep my eyes locked on you so that when I step out in faith in
response to your calling, I will walk on even the most difficult waters
as if my feet were planted on solid ground.*

He Hears

This is the confidence we have in approaching God: that if we ask anything according to his will, he hears us. And if we know that he hears us— whatever we ask—we know that we have what we asked of him.

1 JOHN 5:14-15 NIV

Sometimes it can feel as if God is far away: an elusive man in the heavens who is so far above us that he cannot be interested in our day-to-day lives. Our desires and requests are so small by comparison that it seems unworthy a task to even ask him for help.

But he is a God who loves his children. He wants us to be happy, to feel fulfilled. When we approach him with our wants and needs, he truly hears us! The next time you feel as if your requests are too unimportant to bother God about, remind yourself that he is always listening. Though he may not answer you in the way you expect, he is right there beside you, ready to lend an ear.

God, fill me with your presence today. I know you love me and you want the best for me. Thank you that when I ask, you hear me and you answer.

Held Captive by Fear

When you lie down, you will not be afraid;
Yes, you will lie down and your sleep will be sweet.
Do not be afraid of sudden terror,
Nor of trouble from the wicked when it comes;
For the LORD will be your confidence,
And will keep your foot from being caught.

PROVERBS 3:24-26 NKJV

Fears overwhelm our minds, causing anxious thoughts and sleepless nights. How will the bills get paid this month? Will the doctor have bad news? Family members need help, friends are overwhelmed with suffering, and we can't make it all okay.

When fearful thoughts flood our minds, God's words of wisdom and comfort can get washed away. If we can learn to fully trust him, he will calm our fears and still our quickened hearts. We can be fearless because our confidence is in God and his promises.

Lord Jesus, help me not to be held captive by fear today. Take away the flood of terror and assure me that you are my refuge. You lovingly attend to my every need and I can rest in you.

DAY 55

Truly Special

You are a chosen people, a royal priesthood, a holy nation, God's special possession, that you may declare the praises of him who called you out of darkness into his wonderful light.

1 PETER 2:9 NIV

We all want to believe that we are special. Most of us grow up being told that we are, and it feels good to believe it. But over time, we look around us and realize that, really, we are just like everyone else. Doubt begins to creep in, making us second guess ourselves and damaging our self-confidence.

Long before you were even a wisp in your mother's womb, you were set aside and marked as special. You were chosen to be God's special possession, and that's a pretty amazing thing.

Thank you, God, that you see me as special. I revel in that knowledge today. You call me out of the darkness of the ordinary and bring me into the light of the extraordinary. You have hand-picked me and you love me.

Ordered Steps

I will instruct you in the way you should go;
I will counsel you with my loving eye on you.

PSALM 32:8 NIV

If you've ever taken the hand of a toddler, you'll know that they are relying on you for their balance. If they stumble, you can easily steady them. This simple act of holding a hand means that you and the child have confidence that they won't fall flat on their face!

In the same way, when we commit our way to God, we are essentially placing our hand in his. He delights in the fact that we are walking with him. Even in the times when we stumble, he will steady our path and give us the confidence to keep walking.

Lord, I have stumbled and am sometimes unsure of my walk with you. Give me confidence of your delight in my commitment even though it can be shaky. I accept your hand and continue to walk, trusting you to keep me from falling.

Temptation

Great is our LORD and abundant in strength;
His understanding is infinite.

PSALM 147:5 NASB

When you approach God to ask for help in resisting temptation, or for forgiveness for a sin you've given into, do you feel ashamed? Do you feel like God couldn't possibly understand how you fell into that sin once again?

We know that Jesus was tempted to sin while he was here on earth, but we also know that he never gave into sin. Because he experienced temptation, he has great compassion toward us when we struggle with the desire to sin.

Jesus, you understand my temptation to sin because you were tempted in the same ways! Thank you for being my advocate and understanding how difficult it is to resist temptation. God I ask for your mercy and grace as I continue to submit to you and flee from sin.

DAY 58

Limitless

Again and again they limited God,
preventing him from blessing them.
Continually they turned back from him
and wounded the Holy One!
They forgot his great love, how he took them
by his hand and with redemption's kiss
he delivered them from their enemies.

PSALM 78:41-42 TPT

Do you struggle with where you fit? Are you on a hunt to find your purpose?
Do you feel like you've changed, and the purpose you thought God had for
you seems vastly different now? It can be so confusing, can't it? When we
think our purpose is unclear, we can easily become blind to God's capacity.

Friends, God has no capacity. We serve a God without limits. He tells us that,
in him, anything is possible. You don't need to have confidence in what
you can do—only in what he can accomplish through you. He is capable of
absolutely anything, and his plans for you run deep.

God, I open my heart and mind to the fullness of your love.
Thank you for my purpose in life. Help me walk in a way
that will fulfill that purpose.

Undeniable Trust

"Surely I am with you always, to the very end of the age."
MATTHEW 28:20 NIV

Have you heard a personal story that made you weep? Have you watched as someone overcame undeniable odds and still clung to Jesus? Were you in awe or did you have confidence that you would react the same in a tragedy or difficult situation? Our response to shattered dreams is incredibly important in our spiritual walk. No matter how we feel, our job is to have complete trust and confidence that God is with us, walking right alongside us, holding our hand.

We are called to love him even when it feels like he's not there. We are called to be faithful even when it doesn't feel like he's faithful back. He is. Trusting in God is pleasing to him. He does the rest of the work for us. Isn't that beautiful?

God, I'm facing a tough circumstance and I know I need to press deeper into you. Help me to reach out to you in the hard moments. Your love truly is the best remedy.

Prepare Him Room

"He must become greater and greater,
and I must become less and less."

JOHN 3:30 NLT

Imagine your life if all you ever did was add to your possessions. Unless we want to be featured on a certain, very popular reality television show about people with far too much stuff, bringing new things in necessitates taking old things out. We don't build a bigger closet, we go through and select which items to donate. We don't build a bigger garage, we trade the aging sedan, SUV, or minivan for a newer, better model.

So, too, when we accept Christ's sacrifice and the Holy Spirit takes up residence in our hearts, we must make room. Old habits must make way for fresh, inspired new ways of being. Things like jealousy, bitterness, and insecurity need to be bagged up and taken out so that graciousness, forgiveness, and confidence can move in. As his presence grows inside us, the old ways diminish.

Holy Spirit, help me to allow you all the space in my heart. I don't want to hold back anything for myself. I recognize the need to clean house. I know you will bring about beauty as I do.

Time for Comfort

He comforts us in all our troubles so that we can comfort others.
When they are troubled, we will be able to give them the same
comfort God has given us.

2 CORINTHIANS 1:4 NLT

A young woman sat with head bowed and tears flowing, the heaviness and pain of loss weighing her down. She cried out to the Lord for help as a child cries out for her mother. Almost immediately, God's comfort came. It was as though a tangible weight lifted and a breath of hope settled.

Are you in a time of mourning? Perhaps you've lost a big piece of your life—your job, a friendship, or a loved one. Ecclesiastes tells us, "There is a time to weep and a time to laugh, a time to mourn and a time to dance." In the brief years we spend on this planet, we experience seasons of great joy and seasons when we need God's comfort and peace more than the air we breathe. Can you receive it today? One day, God will use your suffering to bring encouragement and hope to others.

I am so thankful that in my time of sorrow, you offer me comfort. I ask for relief from my heartache and receive it, Lord, in Jesus' name.

Waiting for Dawn

The ransomed of the LORD shall return,
and come to Zion with singing;
everlasting joy shall be upon their heads;
they shall obtain joy and gladness,
and sorrow and sighing shall flee away.

ISAIAH 35:10 NRSV

The sin and sadness of life can make it seem like an endless night, where we are continually waiting for the dawn of Christ's return. In the darkest of nights, it doesn't always help to know that he will return *someday*, because *this day* is full of despair.

To you, his beloved, he gives comfort. Don't lose heart. He is coming for you! It can be hard, because he seems to be taking a long time, but he is preparing a place for you. You are not forgotten in this long night; your pain is familiar to him. Keep your eyes fixed on him! Soon you will hear his voice! He is also longing
for that moment.

Thank you, Jesus, for the promise of your return. It makes difficulties much more bearable when I am assured that one day I will see you, embrace you, and gaze on your beauty!

Overwhelming Devotion

This forever-song I sing of the gentle love of God overwhelming me!
Young and old alike will hear about
your faithful, steadfast love—never failing!
Here's my chorus: "Your mercy grows through the ages.
Your faithfulness is firm, rising up to the skies."

PSALM 89:1-2 TPT

God in his great power and faithfulness never fails us, never gives up on us, and will never leave us alone to fend for ourselves. His love for us remains—regardless of our circumstances or our weaknesses—strong and immovable. His devotion to his children exceeds that of all parents. He is without limits, and nothing can ever change his devotion.

This truth is overwhelmingly satisfying; when such devotion has been proven, what else could attract our gaze? Where else could our eyes find such beauty and purity as they do upon the face of Jesus? In awe, we recognize that his gaze is fixed right back at us, seeing us as a lovely and worthy prize. We can neither deserve this gaze nor escape it. We are flawed, but he is unwavering in his love for us.

Thank you, Father, that you are wholly devoted to me.
Your love is mine to enjoy forever. Help me to remain in that love.

DAY 64

Lifting the Veil

Whenever anyone turns to the Lord,
the veil is taken away.
2 CORINTHIANS 3:16 NIV

Even when we accept Christ as our Savior, there is often a wall that we put up in our hearts. We strive to love him with every fiber of our being, but there can be failure to give him all of us. It's as if the most human part of us feels that by maintaining that last bit of space, we protect ourselves and are free to be who we'd rather be.

True freedom is experienced when we give up, give in, and give ourselves over completely. He wants to take away that veil that prevents us from fully seeing all the beauty that he has in store for us.

God, lift my veil. Take the very last piece of me that has been resisting you. I want to experience the full freedom that you have so gloriously given.

Releasing Beauty

Therefore, since we are surrounded by such a great cloud of witnesses, let us throw off everything that hinders and the sin that so easily entangles.

HEBREWS 12:1 NIV

God provides us relief from any bondage we carry. He truly does. Our Father can take any mistake we've made in the past and release the beauty in that error. We don't need to be so hard on ourselves. We don't need to feel trapped, or think we've failed, or hold on so tightly that we can't see the joy in our current circumstance.

Turn your face toward God and let him break that bondage apart. He can take the journey and form it into a place of humility and empathy for others. Watch as the chains break and you walk away much, much lighter.

God, I have trouble letting go of the mistakes I've made in the past. I thank you for your promise of redemption. I choose today to forgive myself because you have already forgiven me.

You Are Beautiful

You are altogether beautiful, my darling;
there is no flaw in you.

SONG OF SONGS 4:7 NIV

Stereotypes become stereotypes because of the truth in them. We think of a group of girls comparing flaws, calling themselves ugly while reassuring their friends of their beauty. We've heard it. We've lived it. Are you welcoming and accepting of the woman you see in the mirror, or do you analyze, criticize, and judge her?

Let us hear what the Bridegroom says about us. Let us believe the encouraging words of others, and silence the voice in our heads that tells us we are anything but beautiful. The voice is a lie. God's Word is truth, and he says we are beautiful.

Lord, I admit I find it hard to see myself as beautiful sometimes. I choose to look at myself today and smile no matter how difficult it is. I ask that when I do, you will show me how you see me, and help me believe it in my heart.

In Sunshine and Storm

When times are good, be happy;
but when times are bad, consider this:
God has made the one as well as the other.
Therefore, no one can discover
anything about their future.

ECCLESIASTES 7:14 NIV

It's easy to feel happy on a sunny day, when all is well, the birds are singing, and life is going along swimmingly. But what happens when waters are rougher, bad news comes, or the days feel just plain hard?

God wants us to feel gladness when times are good. He has made each and every day. We are called to rejoice in all of them whether good or bad. Happiness is determined by our circumstances, but true joy comes when we can find the silver linings, hidden in our darkest hours—when we can sing his praises no matter what. We don't know what the future holds for us here on earth, but we can find our delight in the knowledge that our eternity is set in beauty.

God, I don't want my happiness to be determined by my circumstance. Help me discover true joy in you. Give me a deep and abiding satisfaction in each day that goes beyond human understanding.

Lighthouses

"You are the light of the world. A town built on a hill cannot be hidden.
Neither do people light a lamp and put it under a bowl. Instead they put it
on its stand, and it gives light to everyone in the house."

MATTHEW 5:14-15 NIV

There's a good reason why lighthouses were built. For hundreds of years,
they've shined brightly across harbors around the world, guiding ships
safely to shore. The premise was simple; put the light up high where
it can easily be seen.

Jesus is the light of the world. That light wasn't meant to be hidden away.
It's meant to be put up high, where everyone can easily see it. And as his
followers, we are called to shine brightly for him, in such a way that others
can see it for themselves. We don't hide it away;
we boldly light the way to Christ.

*God, help me not to hide my light. Give me boldness of faith to
be a source of light for everyone who comes in contact with me.
I want to shine brightly so others can step out of darkness and join
me in your marvelous light.*

Like You Mean It

"'If you can'?" said Jesus.
"Everything is possible for one who believes."

MARK 9:23 NIV

When you pray, are you doing it in a spirit of boldness, or are you praying weak prayers? It's as if we are afraid to bother God with our requests. For goodness sake, we better not pester him too much, or perhaps he won't answer them at all, right? So we speak tentatively, "Dear Lord, if it is your will, it'd be great if you could..." "Father, I know you have so much on your plate, but I'd love it if...."

Stop with the weak prayers. The Lord knows your heart already. Believe that he can do what you are asking. There is no need for caution with the Father who loves you so dearly. Jesus said so himself. Step out boldly in faith, beginning with your prayer life.

God, help me overcome my unbelief. I want to believe that everything is possible because I believe in you.

Pieced Together

Hallelujah! Praise the Lord!
How beautiful it is when we sing our praises
to the beautiful God;
for praise makes you lovely before him
and brings him great delight!
He heals the wounds of every shattered heart.

PSALM 147:1, 3 TPT

Whether you are carrying pain and suffering from past abuse or tragedy, or you've more recently been hurt, run toward the one who heals. There is no requirement or need too great; he will piece you back together.

It might take work. It will take constant communion with him to remind you of his healing power, but he will glue you back until you are whole. Broken souls, broken bodies, broken relationships, be reminded of his power in these moments and do not turn away.

Father God, I am in need of your healing power.
I release everything I am holding on to and
ask for you to heal my wounds.

Your Heart's Desire

Make God the utmost delight and pleasure of your life,
and he will provide for you what you desire the most.

PSALM 37:4 TPT

What did you want more than anything else in the world when you were little? Maybe having a pony or being a princess were the most delightful things you could imagine back then. What do you yearn for now? How different are your adult dreams?

We've all heard that God loves to answer our prayers and to grant our desires. Should we expect him, then, to give us whatever we want? Study the verse above, and notice in particular the first part. *When we make God the utmost delight of our life* he gives us the desires of our heart. If we delight in financial success, washboard abs, or highly accomplished children, he makes no promises. This does not mean we are wrong for wanting these, just that God isn't necessarily invested in making them happen for us.

God, help me to make you the utmost delight and pleasure in my life.
I want my desires to be your desires. I want my heart to
feel your heart.

DAY 72

Weary to the Core

The steps of the God-pursuing ones
follow firmly in the footsteps of the Lord.
And God delights in every step they take to follow him.
If they stumble badly they will still survive,
for the Lord lifts them up with his hands.

PSALM 37:23-24 TPT

Have you ever been run so ragged that you just didn't know if you could take even one more step? Your calendar is a blur of scheduled activities, your days are full, your every hour is blocked off for this or that, and it's hard to find even a spare minute for yourself. Even your very bones feel weary, and you fall into your bed at night, drained from it all.

There is someone who is ready to catch you when you fall. You might stumble throughout your busy day, but he will never let you hit the floor as you take a tumble. God delights in you! He will direct your every step if you ask him to. He will gladly take you by the hand and guide you.

Lord, please guide my days! I am weary and I need your energy to get through all that this day holds. Help me take your hand and let you walk me through each day, fully trusting you to provide the strength I need.

Choosing Wisdom

If you wait at wisdom's doorway,
longing to hear a word for every day,
joy will break forth within you as you listen
for what I'll say.
For the fountain of life pours into you every time
that you find me,
and this is the secret of growing in the delight
and the favor of the Lord.

PROVERBS 8:34-36 TPT

The word *wisdom* is used hundreds of times in the Bible. Time and time again, we are instructed to use good judgement, to make sound decisions, to use prudence and circumspection.

King Solomon made a special point to ask God to give him wisdom throughout his time as Israel's leader. Because of this, God honored and blessed him.

God, I choose wisdom today! I wait at wisdom's doorway.
I know true happiness is found there.

Cheer for the Prize

May the God who gives endurance and encouragement give you the same
attitude of mind toward each other that Christ Jesus had.

ROMANS 15:5 NIV

Have you ever watched cheerleaders at a sporting event? Smiling, bubbly,
energetic, yelling for their beloved team. What we don't see is what might
be going on underneath all of that encouragement. Everyone has their
issues. And yet there they are, faithfully devoted to their team because they
know the prize at the end.

In this same way, let us encourage one another in our faith. Imagine our
Abba Father's joy when he sees us lifting each other up in praise and loving
despite whatever we might have going on. There is so much to be gained
in relationship with other believers whether on the receiving or giving end.
And the prize at the end is eternity. There is nothing greater.

God, show me ways in which I can encourage others. I know it
delights your heart when you see me giving my time and talents—
and that makes it more than worth it!

Let God Win

Truthful words stand the test of time,
but lies are soon exposed.

PROVERBS 12:19 NLT

Don't believe the lies. There is an enemy out there who wants to steal, kill, and destroy. One of the most powerful ways he does that is through filling our hearts with things we think are true about ourselves. Those lies fill our minds with hatred, so that when we look in the mirror, we start hating what we see. *I'm so ugly. I don't deserve anything good in my life. I screwed up again; why do I even try?*

These thoughts make the Father weep. He loves us! He knits us together and sets us apart. He cherishes every breath we take, and in the name of Jesus, we can rebuke the enemy so those lies no longer fill our heads and overtake our hearts.

Jesus, lift the veil from my eyes so I can see clearly. Show me the lies I am believing that are destructive. I know you love me and you want to see me walk in truth.

Confident in Incompetence

It is not that we think we are qualified to do anything on our own. Our qualification comes from God.

2 CORINTHIANS 3:5 NLT

Whether bringing a brand new baby home from the hospital, giving your first major presentation at work, or simply making your first Thanksgiving meal, there's probably been at least one moment in your life that had you thinking, *I have no idea what I'm doing. I'm not qualified.* So what did you do? Chances are, you put a smile on your face, dove in, and did your best.

The older we get, the more we realize how truly helpless we are. We also, beautifully, realize it's okay. There is great freedom in admitting our shortcomings and allowing the Father to be our strength. No matter what he asks of us, we are confident in our incompetence. We may not be capable, but God is more than qualified to carry out his plans through us. All we need to do is swallow our pride and let him lead us.

*Lord God, I want to embrace your competence as my own,
so my dreams and my calling can be fulfilled.
I swallow my pride and ask you to lead me.*

Surrender Your Heart

O my son, give me your heart.
May your eyes take delight in following my ways.
PROVERBS 23:26 NLT

Watching the news we learn the losing army in a war has surrendered to their enemy. The fugitive has finally surrendered to police after a long standoff. Perhaps, closer to home, someone you know has surrendered to addiction. So how, given all these examples, are we supposed to feel good about surrendering to God? Allowing ourselves to be vulnerable can be scary. Doesn't *surrender* mean defeat, giving up?

It would... if God were our enemy. But because he is for us and not against us, surrender means something else altogether. It means *freedom*. Surrender also means abandoning ourselves to God and no longer resisting him—accepting his plans and his perfect will for our lives. We don't have to strive any more once we give him our hearts.

Father, help me remember that your plans are perfect,
and that your will for me is peace. I surrender my whole heart
to you and end the struggle of holding on. I trust you with
my heart because you are good.

Conscious Choice

"Today I have given you the choice between life and death,
between blessings and curses. Now I call on heaven and earth
to witness the choice you make. Oh, that you would choose life,
so that you and your descendants might live!"

DEUTERONOMY 30:19 NLT

Would you want someone to love you if they didn't really want to? If someone were forced or even paid to love you but you knew their love wasn't genuine, would you enjoy that type of love?

We have the conscious ability to choose whether or not we will love God. God will not make us love him or force us to follow him. The freedom that we have to choose is the most wonderful *and* the most fearful gift we have been given.

God, I choose life. I know you have wonderful things waiting for me as I respond to your love. I worship you with all that I am.

Uncomplicated Freedom

I have swept away your offenses like a cloud,
your sins like the morning mist.
Return to me, for I have redeemed you.

ISAIAH 44:22 NIV

We over-complicate freedom in the Christian life. Through our legalisms, we try to find a way to humanize the redeeming work of the cross because we simply can't wrap our minds around the supernatural character of God.

It can be hard to understand the complete grace offered at Calvary because we are incapable of giving that kind of grace. But when God says that he has forgotten our sin, and that he has made us new, he really means it. God is love, and love keeps no record of wrongs. Nothing can keep us from his love. Salvation tore the veil that separated us from the holiness of God. That complete work cannot be diminished or erased by anything we do.

Thank you, God, that freedom is truly simple.
The beauty of your gospel is summed up in the
single concept of grace, undeserved and given
without restraint. I accept it today.

My Reward

"I will bring the blind by a way they did not know;
I will lead them in paths they have not known.
I will make darkness light before them,
And crooked places straight.
These things I will do for them,
And not forsake them."

ISAIAH 42:16 NKJV

Spring is a time of rebirth and renewal, a reward for making it through the long, cold, desolate winter. Some parts of the world have enjoyed colorful spring gardens in full fragrant bloom for weeks. In other regions, the cold snow is still melting and the earliest bulbs have yet to reach through the hard soil. Whether above the surface or below, resurrection is happening all around us, rewarding us with new life and vitality. Resurrection is a revival of hope, of light shining in the darkness, of our glorious reward.

Isaiah 42:16 shares a promise that cannot be taken away from us. He has achieved his glory and we will share in its reward: death cannot conquer or steal our inheritance! Therefore, we can fully trust and believe in Jesus Christ, our hope. There is nothing more magnificent, nothing else worthy of our expectations!

God, thank you for your gift of salvation. Let the sin that has hindered me melt away like the winter snow. I believe that today will be full of promise and life.

The Need to Breathe

When hard pressed, I cried to the LORD;
he brought me into a spacious place.

PSALM 118:5 NIV

There are days, aren't there, when the walls really do seem to be closing in? Pressed from every side with needs, obligations, expectations, and commitments, you wonder not just how, but *if* you can keep it all together. When do you get to breathe?

The book of Psalms is filled with such pressures, often in the form of angry armies hoping to kill King David. What was his unfailing response? Prayer. What a wonderful image: a spacious place! Take your pressures to the Lord, and feel them lift; feel your surroundings and your hope expand. Catch your breath with the one gave you life.

Lord, you see the pressures of my everyday life.
I want to stop and catch my breath with you in
the spacious place. Only in those moments will
the stresses lift and peace settle.

Remain in Me

> "I am the true vine, and My Father is the vinedresser. Every branch in Me that does not bear fruit, He takes away; and every branch that bears fruit, He prunes it so that it may bear more fruit.... I am the vine, you are the branches; he who abides in Me and I in him, he bears much fruit, for apart from Me you can do nothing."
>
> JOHN 15:1-2, 5 NASB

Jesus gives a wonderfully life-giving illustration. He is the vine, God is the vinedresser, and we are the branches. We know that a vinedresser's job is incredibly important. A plant will never bear as much fruit without a vinedresser as it would with one.

God says that the only thing we need to do to bear fruit is to remain in the vine. That is a nice, simple task. If we stay in the vine, he promises to nurture us and sustain us. He also promises to prune us. The pruning isn't for the sake of staying small. It is so we can bear even more fruit.

Father, knowing that you have my best interest in mind makes it easier to submit willingly to your pruning. Help me to remain in you so you can do what you need to keep me bearing fruit.

Working with Purpose

Whatever you do, do well. For when you go
to the grave, there will be no work or planning
or knowledge or wisdom.

ECCLESIASTES 9:10 NLT

Every day you wake up is a new opportunity to put everything you are into your work—whether that work is inside your home or out. You should put your heart and soul into your efforts. You may not like where you are in life, but you were given today, so take advantage of it!

We don't always like the task we are assigned or the jobs that we need to do. Regardless of where you are and what you do, give it your best. There is no reward in not trying, but there is joy and a sense of satisfaction in working hard.

God, help me to give my all in every opportunity ahead of me today. Even if I don't like I what I am doing, I thank you that you have called me to this place and you will help me work with purpose.

DAY 84

Our Father in Heaven

The eyes of the LORD are on the righteous,
and his ears are attentive to their cry.
PSALM 34:15 NIV

Do we know in the depths of our hearts that our prayers are heard:
both the shouting cries for help and the gentle whispers of thanksgiving?
He knows our every thought before we even think it. This is the Father
that created us. This is the Abba that calls us by name. We are his beloved
children.

We need to let the truth sink into the very deepest parts of our hearts and
rest there in thanksgiving. His Word is truth, and he tells us time and time
again that he will answer our prayer because we trust in him. Whether
through song, action, thought, or speech, he delights in hearing our
prayers.

God, it is truly amazing to me that you delight in hearing from me.
That you would tune in to what I am saying because you are
interested in my heart is something that is hard for me to fathom.
What a wonderfully good God you are.

The Call for Help

I look up to the hills,
but where does my help come from?
My help comes from the LORD,
who made heaven and earth.

PSALM 121:1-2 NCV

Depending on the type of person you are, you may not be very good at asking for help. There are those who like to be the *helpers*: they do best serving others because they feel capable and useful. Then there are those who gladly accept service any time they are given the opportunity. Neither is better than the other, and both have their positive elements.

In different seasons of life, natural helpers may need to be the ones receiving help. Sometimes this is hard to accept, and we have to be careful not to let pride take control. Asking for help is part of being vulnerable: we push everything aside to say, "I can't do this alone." God has put capable people in our lives who love to help, but they won't know we need help until we ask.

Father, show me when I'm being stubborn in not asking for help. I trust you to place people in my life who can both share my burdens and allow me to help them with theirs.

Risk-taker

Your word is a lamp to guide my feet
and a light for my path.
PSALM 119:105 NLT

There will be opportunities that arise that might be surprising to us. We might suddenly be presented with something that feels kind of terrifying. We view it as an opportunity because we see the benefit in it somewhere along the way. We understand that it could be as much of a gift to our lives as a potentially difficult ride or transition before the gift appears.

Stepping through the unknown takes courage, and courage isn't always readily available. Through the power of prayer, and wrestling with the opportunity's positives and negatives, hopefully we come to the point where our hearts feel the peace we've been looking for. That makes the task of accepting the opportunity much easier. You still might not feel brave about a decision, but you can trust the peace in your heart. That alone takes courage.

God, with every new opportunity that arises, help me to seek you for wisdom and peace in how to approach it. You know what I should go after and what I should leave alone. I trust in your peace to guide me.

Rolled Away

> When they looked up, they saw that the stone, which was very large,
> had been rolled away. "You are looking for Jesus the Nazarene, who was
> crucified. He has risen! He is not here. See the place where they laid him."
>
> MARK 16:4, 6 NIV

Most of us know that Jesus was raised from the dead. Whenever we hear it, we know it to be part of the story of Jesus. But have we ever really meditated on the truth of that statement? Jesus was raised from the dead! Certainly he can be trusted with our lives.

Many times we doubt God's love for us. We cast him aside and try to do it all ourselves. We doubt his truth and his healing power. We don't think we can do everything through his strength, yet, in the same breath, we easily accept that Jesus died and rose again. If he can do that, our trials can be overcome!

Thank you for the reminder, Jesus, that the stone was rolled away! I
believe it, and I believe that all of your promises are true.
You love me! I can trust you with all of the details that I have
been trying to control.

DAY 88

Not Afraid of Aging

That is why we never give up. Though our bodies are dying,
our spirits are being renewed every day.

2 CORINTHIANS 4:16 NLT

Aging is part of life. It's funny how the aging process seems to start so
slowly and then later in life it gets faster and faster. It would be easy to
lose heart if we gauged our aging experience purely by what we saw in the
mirror. If we did that, we might begin to fear or
hate the aging process.

As we abide with the Lord, aging means we are also maturing. We grow
in strength and grace in our knowledge of him. We might not look like we
used to, but we also aren't being tossed about. There are many benefits
to growing older in Jesus. We are not meant to stay young forever. We are
eternal beings that will exist eternally. Because of this, we don't need to
despise aging. God is preparing for us an eternal weight of glory beyond all
comparison.

As I age, God, give me your perspective.
The world doesn't do me any favors in this regard. Remind me that
maturity is eternally beautiful, and this world is only temporal.

Shower of Love

Love never gives up,
never loses faith,
is always hopeful,
and endures through
every circumstance.

1 CORINTHIANS 13:7 NLT

Everyone makes mistakes. So, be kind to yourself. Be kind to the person you see in the mirror, to the one you might not think is worthy of love. God loves you, inadequacies and all. He sees you through the lens of a Father that loves without conditions or expectations.

We can learn so much from the love of our heavenly Father. It is important to make every effort to see beyond the situation in front of us. We can choose to look for the best in ourselves and in others—giving grace and loving unconditionally through every circumstance.

Thank you, Father, for your love that never fails. Even though I make mistakes, you see past those and continue to delight in me. Help me to learn from your example.

The Letter

O my people, trust in him at all times.
Pour out your heart to him,
for God is our refuge.

PSALM 62:8 NLT

It is always good to have a confidante: someone we can unload on without fear of rejection or criticism. To Christians, God offers himself as that person. There is a story told in 2 Kings that illustrates this truth. King Hezekiah of Judah was a God-fearing king who did what was pleasing in God's sight. His enemy, the king of Assyria, began a campaign to instill fear in the people by mocking their faith in God. When King Hezekiah received a letter threatening annihilation, he took that letter and spread it out before the Lord. He poured his heart out to God, praying for deliverance, and God miraculously rescued them.

Our God is waiting for us to pour out our hearts to him. Go ahead; write out your concerns and burdens, and spread your letter out before the Lord. He is our refuge. He will take our worries and concerns and hide us away in safety.

Thank you, Lord, for the invitation to pour out my heart to you. Here are my burdens—I relinquish them to you and trust you with them.

The Morning Cry

In the morning, LORD, you hear my voice;
in the morning I lay my requests before you
and wait expectantly.

PSALM 5:3 NIV

The day dawns cloudy and bleak, but the tasks that lie ahead pay no mind to the weather. The days run together endlessly, and this one promises nothing different. Job, sickness, and financial problems are there waiting in the early hours. It was perhaps on a morning like this, when David cried out to the Lord.

What an amazing comfort to know that no matter how gray the moment, it is not our job to fret or figure it out. Rather, we can pour out our need to the Father, lay the burden on him, and go about our business. Waiting is not passive; it's active as we proceed through our day confident of God's faithfulness.

O Lord, this morning I lift my needs and burdens to you. I rise to meet the day knowing you have heard me and will order my steps.

The Faithfulness of God

Let us draw near to God with a sincere heart and with the full assurance
that faith brings, having our hearts sprinkled to cleanse us from a guilty
conscience and having our bodies washed with pure water.
Let us hold unswervingly to the hope we profess,
for he who promised is faithful.

HEBREWS 10:22-23 NIV

God is good and he knows all of your needs. He is faithful and he longs to
show you more of his glory and beauty. Prepare your heart to say "yes" to
his call. Trust in his faithfulness. Chase after his joy.

Your love is pleasing to him because he delights in you. He sings over you,
notes and refrains here and there as you walk the earth, waiting for him.
One day, his song will be complete, and when you hear its fullness, you will
run to him! Until that day, trust in his faithfulness. *Hold unswervingly to the
hope you profess* because you have *the full assurance that faith brings;* your
heart is cleansed and you are pure.

**In so many ways, God, you have demonstrated
your faithfulness in my life. Thank you for your
sacrifice that has cleansed me and has given me hope.**

Sufficient Grace

God is so rich in mercy, and he loved us so much, that even though we were dead because of our sins, he gave us life when he raised Christ from the dead. (It is only by God's grace that you have been saved!)… God saved you by his grace when you believed. And you can't take credit for this; it is a gift from God. Salvation is not a reward for the good things we have done, so none of us can boast about it.

EPHESIANS 2:4-5, 8-9 NLT

There is no greater education in the amazing grace of God than his own words. When the impact of his grace has saved you, these words have a particularly powerful and humbling effect. We have done nothing, yet we have everything. We were dead but now we have life. We didn't pay with money, flesh, or enslavement. We just believed.

We cannot boast in our salvation, but we can sing praises from the rafters for this amazing gift. Sing long and loud, for grace is the one and only gift we will ever need. And we can share it, without losing an ounce of our portion. It multiplies over and over, as long as we are willing to give it away. We know beyond a shadow of doubt that his grace is sufficient for us. It has been from the moment we first believed!

***Thank you, God, for your undeserved gift of grace.
I am in awe of you.***

Walking Honorably

The name of the Lord Jesus will be honored because of the way you live, and you will be honored along with him. This is all made possible because of the grace of our God and Lord, Jesus Christ.

2 THESSALONIANS 1:12 NLT

Honor awards are usually given to those who achieve excellence in specific fields. People are honored for their performance in musical, athletic, academic, and professional arenas. Some are honored for their exceptional bravery or intelligence. And rightly so. But if honor is given only for excellent achievement, how on earth can we be considered honorable with our less-than-impressive abilities?

The secret to living a life that honors God is found in depending heavily on his grace to cover us. We keep it simple. We do what we know is right. We don't compromise. We don't chase after the shiny honor awards of the world. And when we get it wrong, we humbly admit our failure, accept God's forgiveness, and keep walking the narrow road.

God, no honor award is worth seeking after unless it will bring honor to you. I am so human, and you are so perfect, I can't even begin to achieve the excellence standard you require. But by your grace, you have made me able and consider me worthy.

Hope in God

May the God of hope fill you with all joy and peace as you trust in him, so that you may overflow with hope by the power of the Holy Spirit.

ROMANS 15:13 NIV

I hope it doesn't rain today. I hope I did well on that final. I hope he didn't forget our anniversary. I hope I get a promotion. Few things that we hope for contain the kind of satisfaction that lasts. Even if we get what we hoped for, what comes next? We have to hope for something else. And while it's not bad to hope for these, the truth is that any of them are disappointing if not met, and all of them only carry temporary satisfaction.

The one thing we can hope for that has lasting value is our eternity with the Lord. And that's actually exciting! Think of life without fear, pain, guilt, sorrow, sickness, loss, rejection, or death. Think about an abundance of love, joy, peace, kindness, and beauty. When we choose to put our hope in God, we will not be disappointed. Our expectations will be *exceeded.* How often does *that* happen?

**God, I see how hope in earthly things is only temporary.
I put my hope instead in the eternal reward of living forever with you.
That is so much more exciting!**

The Word Is Alive

The word of God is alive and powerful. It is sharper than the sharpest two-edged sword, cutting between soul and spirit, between joint and marrow. It exposes our innermost thoughts and desires.

HEBREWS 4:12 NLT

Have you ever opened your Bible to a random page and been amazed that the Scripture passage is perfectly appropriate for that exact season of your life? Then at church your pastor uses the same verse as the basis for a sermon. While driving a few days later, a worship song's lyrics match up again to your life. It's like God has a spotlight on you and is aligning the world around you to encourage, direct, or teach you wherever you are. His Word is truly *alive and powerful*!

The Word of God is a marvelously insightful gift. He gave it for our edification, education, and inspiration. Whatever we are going through, the Word of God holds the answer. Whether we are running away from God or toward him, whether we are rejoicing or mourning, however confused or secure we feel, God's Word holds the solution.

God, thank you for your Word that is alive and powerful.
Thank you for using it to speak into my life,
to bring hope and encouragement when I need it most.

A Person of Integrity

Teach me your decrees, O LORD;
I will keep them to the end.
Give me understanding and I will obey your instructions;
I will put them into practice with all my heart.
Make me walk along the path of your commands,
for that is where my happiness is found.

PSALM 119:33-35 NLT

Adventurous Hollywood tales of heroes have little in common with reality, except, perhaps, the hero. Heroes really do exist. They serve us coffee or walk their dogs down our street. Maybe you are a hero. It doesn't take much really, just being in the right place at the right time. And, of course, doing the right thing. This is what sets a hero apart: a hero does the right thing.

Heroes put aside their own desires and interests. They have integrity, which means they do what most people wouldn't take the time, risk, or effort to do. David's psalm reads like an oath, a decree for heroes everywhere, spoken as a promise to uphold the integrity of God's goodness and righteousness. How can you be a hero? By learning God's commands and keeping them.

Lord, show me what it means to walk with integrity.
I submit to walking your path, knowing that you will put me
in the right place at the right time. And obedience
to you always leads to joy in the end.

The Judge

I will proclaim the name of the LORD;
ascribe greatness to our God!
"The Rock, his work is perfect, for all his ways are justice.
A God of faithfulness and without iniquity,
just and upright is he."

DEUTERONOMY 32:3-4 ESV

Being a judge is a weighty calling; if you've ever had to judge a children's art competition, you might understand. Lovingly crafted, covered in heavy-handed brush strokes, glitter, and smiling stick figures, the smudged papers are held below smiling, expectant faces. *Which one is the best?* Could anyone choose a winner, and at the same time create a loser?

Thankfully, God is great and perfect—two qualities you want in a judge. He alone is qualified to judge mankind. He alone will bring about justice with his mighty hand, and it will be eternal. Because he is faithful and without wickedness, we can rest without worry. Have faith in this as well: *his work is perfect.* His works of compassion, love, healing, and grace are perfect. And his ways of justice are perfect. He will make everything right one day.

God, I admit I find it difficult to wait for your justice.
At times I want to take it into my own hands and
judge from my human understanding. Help me to
trust that your judgment is perfect.

Don't Walk Away

"All the bridesmaids got up and prepared their lamps. Then the five foolish ones asked the others, 'Please give us some of your oil because our lamps are going out.' But the others replied, 'We don't have enough for all of us. Go to a shop and buy some for yourselves.' But while they were gone to buy oil, the bridegroom came. Then those who were ready went in with him to the marriage feast, and the door was locked."

MATTHEW 25:7-10 NLT

In the days leading up to Jesus' return, many believers will walk away. The ones who are unprepared for the pain, suffering, and sacrifice of those days will leave the truth. Their faith, under severe testing, will falter. Their lamps will go out. It's a warning for us all.

Begin filling your lamp with the oil of faith now, so that in the hour of Christ's return you will not walk away. Only by faith will we make it through the night; faith is the oil that keeps the lamp lit. Our perseverance depends on our preparation. Have you stored up enough oil for that long night? Or will you have to walk away, unprepared, before the bridegroom's return? By faith and faith alone, you will not walk away!

God, I choose to fill my lamp and many extra vessels with the oil of faith, so that even if the night is long, my oil will not run out. I do not want to walk away from you when times are difficult.

My First Love

I know you are enduring patiently and bearing up for my name's sake,
and you have not grown weary. But I have this against you, that you have
abandoned the love you had at first. Remember therefore from where you
have fallen; repent, and do the works you did at first.

REVELATION 2:3-5 ESV

All we need is you, Lord. What can the world offer us that will not perish?
What can the world give that can withstand God's refining fire? When we
are tested, everything else will fall away. Only our love for him will remain.
Our salvation cannot be stolen from us. God's love for us cannot
be quenched.

Remember the early days of your walk with Jesus? The way your eyes
were opened to understanding, how your heart was broken in love, your
arms were lifted in praise, and your knees bent in repentance? God wants
that. He misses the desperation you had for him, the focused time you
spent in his Word, and the joy you found in prayer. His love for you has not
diminished. Can you find your first love again?

God, I want you to be my first love.
I want to remember the love I had for you at first
and walk in that love. You are really all I need.

God's Timing

We are saved by trusting. And trusting means looking forward to getting something we don't yet have—for a man who already has something doesn't need to hope and trust that he will get it. But if we must keep trusting God for something that hasn't happened yet, it teaches us to wait patiently and confidently.

ROMANS 8:24-25 TLB

It's hard to wait for, well, anything. We can have almost anything we want immediately. Sometimes even waiting longer than two days to receive our order in the mail seems way too long. We can gain some great perspective when we think about how life was lived hundreds or even thousands of years ago. Mail took months to travel, items were all made to order, and food was only delivered to your doorway if it accompanied out-of-town guests. We have become pretty impatient, haven't we?

It's hard to wait for God's timing. Even when we are waiting for *good* things, we think we shouldn't have to wait for long. Going on a missions trip, starting a job in ministry, leading a small group, marrying the right person… doesn't God want those things for us sooner rather than later? Trusting in God's timing means you believe that God won't let an opportunity slip by unless it's not one he wants you to experience.

Father, I admit it is hard for me to wait for anything.
Help me to be patient and trust that you will give me
everything I need when I need it.

Free To Do What

You, my brothers and sisters, were called to be free. But do not use your freedom to indulge the flesh; rather, serve one another humbly in love.

GALATIANS 5:13 NIV

What would you do with a day of total freedom? All your obligations, limitations, and commitments are lifted. Do you head to a spa, shop 'til you drop, party like it's 1999? If we're being honest, most of us considered something along these lines.

Our challenge as children of the Almighty is to see freedom a different way. Paul admonishes the Galatians to look at the liberty they have because of Christ's sacrifice not as a license to indulge, but to reach out. Free of the restrictions of the Old Testament law, we needn't concern ourselves with having a clean slate, or making sure our neighbors do. We are free to meet the needs we see around us—to openly, freely love one another.

Lord, show me how I can best serve others. Help me to use my freedom not to indulge in my own selfish desires, but to give of myself to those around me.

New Life

The LORD is good to all,
and his mercy is over all that he has made.

PSALM 145:9 ESV

Have you ever laid in bed at night, thinking over past wrongdoings and beating yourself up over decisions you made years ago? If so, you are not alone. We can be incredibly hard on ourselves, asking for near perfection.

There is good news for us all! Once we accept Christ as our Savior, we are made new. There is no need to continue to berate ourselves for the choices of the past. He has washed away our sins and made us clean.
We don't have to look at life from our former point of view because our old lives are gone and new ones have begun!

Lord, I release my past to you. Help me forgive myself for past mistakes and realize that you have made me new. I want to walk in this freedom today.

Perfect

His divine power has granted to us everything pertaining to life and
godliness, through the true knowledge of Him who called us
by His own glory and excellence.

2 PETER 1:3 NASB

Each of us is keenly aware of our own weaknesses. We know all of our flaws
too well and we make eliminating them our goal. But no matter how much
effort we put out, we can never and will never achieve perfection.

Despite most of us realizing that we will never be perfect, we still put
unreasonable pressure on ourselves. Whether in a task, in our character, or
in our walk with Christ, we easily become frustrated when we reach
for perfection and can't grasp it. But if we allow perfectionism to drive
our performance, then we will quench our own potential and inhibit
our effectiveness.

God, you give me the freedom to not be perfect.
Your power is all the more perfect when displayed
in my weakness. Thank you that when I mess up,
you take over.

Grace upon Grace

For of His fullness we have all received,
and grace upon grace.
JOHN 1:16 NASB

You know those days, the perfect ones? Your hair looks great, you nail a work assignment (whether client presentation, spreadsheet, or getting twins to nap at the same time), you say just the right thing and make someone's day, and then come home to find dinner waiting for you. It's good upon good, blessing upon blessing.

Being a child of the Almighty gains us access to that blessed feeling every day, even when our circumstances are ordinary or difficult. His love is so full, and his grace so boundless, that when his Spirit lives in us, even a flat tire can feel like a blessing. Our status as beloved children of the King guarantees it!

God, I see your grace poured out today
and I thank you for it.

The Spirit Is Willing

I know that nothing good dwells in me, that is,
in my flesh; for the willing is present in me,
but the doing of the good is not.
ROMANS 7:18 NASB

Lord, I know the right thing to do, but I just don't have the strength to do it. This thought has likely been on our minds more often than we want to admit. We don't like to acknowledge that sometimes we just don't have it in us to make the right choice.

Paul understood the internal conflict that we face in doing right. As new creations in Christ, we have in us the desire to do good; however, as part of a fallen world, we are inherently selfish. In which direction do we position ourselves? We can dwell on our desire to do right, or on our desire to please ourselves. The more we set our minds in the right direction, the easier it will become.

Above all, God, help me remember that it is the enabling power of Christ that I must rely on to continue to make the right decisions; it is through your grace that I can overcome.

Vulnerability

He gives us more grace. That is why Scripture says:
"God opposes the proud
but shows favor to the humble."
JAMES 4:6 NIV

Some of the most substantial and ultimately wonderful changes in our lives come from moments of vulnerability: laying our cards on the table, so to speak, and letting someone else know how much they really mean to us. But vulnerability takes one key ingredient: humility. And humility is not an easy pill to swallow.

Isn't it sometimes easier for us to pretend that conflict never happened than to face the fact that we made a mistake and wronged another person? It's not always easy to humble ourselves and fight for the resolution in an argument—especially when it means admitting our failures. Who are you in the face of conflict? Do you avoid apologizing in an attempt to save face? Does your pride get in the way of vulnerability, or are you willing and ready to humble yourself for restoration in your relationships?

God, you say that you will give favor and wisdom to the humble.
I humble myself today for the sake of restoring a relationship.
Show me exactly how to do that.

DAY 108

All Things Are Possible

It is God who makes us able to do all that we do.

2 CORINTHIANS 12:9 ESV

In the midst of trying situations, there are days when we're so exhausted we feel like we can barely put one foot in front of the other. The thought of creating some semblance of a meal, or even getting out of bed for that matter, seems near impossible. Forget about responding gracefully when people say or do ridiculous things. Forget about the project that was supposed to be finished two weeks ago. Forget about going to that event we thought we wanted to attend. We just *can't* keep up.

The good news is God doesn't expect us to. In fact, he doesn't even want us to. When we allow ourselves to be weak in our grief-filled moments, we give God the opportunity to show his strength—and he'll take that opportunity every time we give it to him. We don't have to be "willing and able"; we can just be willing because *God* is able.

Lord, I give you all the tasks that seem impossible today. Rest on me in my weakness and give me the strength I need to do what really needs to be done. Help me also to say no to the things that can wait.

He Is Real

His divine power has given us everything we need for a godly life through
our knowledge of him who called us by his own glory and goodness.
Through these he has given us his very great and precious promises.

2 PETER 1:3-4 NIV

The test for authenticity is often measured by applying some kind of force
or foreign substance to that which is being tested. Determining whether
something is made of real gold can be accomplished in a number of ways.
Perhaps the most simple is by rubbing the gold on an unglazed ceramic
plate. The color of the mark left on the plate determines the authenticity of
the gold. Real gold will leave a gold mark. Fake gold will leave a black mark.
You can see the analogy, can't you?

At some time in our lives, we will undergo an authenticity test. We might be
put through several—daily. What mark will we leave when we encounter
those tests? When we brush up against difficulty? If we are authentic
Christians, the mark we leave will be gold—the true mark of Christ.

*God, you are real, and you are good. You have given us an example
of how to remain authentic in a world full of fraud and deception.
Thank you for your great and precious promises. I press on
in your strength today.*

Approach with Confidence

So let us come boldly to the throne of our gracious God. There we will receive his mercy, and we will find grace to help us when we need it most.

HEBREWS 4:16 NLT

Imagine walking into Buckingham Palace, unnoticed and unrestricted, without knocking or announcing yourself, and pulling up a chair alongside Her Majesty, the Queen of England. "I've had such a long day. Nothing has gone right, and now my car is making the strangest noise. Could you help me out?"

Such an image is almost absurd! There is a protocol to seeing royalty— many rules to follow, not to mention the armed guards protecting every side. But there is a royal throne we can approach without fear or proper etiquette. It is without guards, payments, locks, and restrictions. Its occupant is the God of all creation, and he is eager to hear about your day's ups and downs.

God, I approach your throne of grace and lift up my voice to you. I know that you love my company and you want to hear what I have to say. I ask you to supply everything I need, and guide me in the way that you know is best for me.

The Compassionate One

The LORD is compassionate and gracious,
Slow to anger and abounding in lovingkindness.
PSALM 103:8 NASB

Consider the Israelites wandering in the desert: God had rescued them out of bondage and went before them in a pillar of fire, providing for their every need and protecting them. What did they offer to him? Complaints.

Listen to the psalms of David—the man after God's own heart—as he lays his burdens at the feet of God, praising his majesty and might. But what did David do when he wanted what he could not have? Stole, murdered, and lied.

Paul, who gave his life to preach the gospel he loved to people near and far, shared the astounding gift of God's grace to Jews and Gentiles alike. But who was he before his conversion? A hateful, persecuting murderer of Christians.

God loves his children regardless of their sin, their past, and their failings. This love is poured out on us with consideration and patience. We aren't dealt with as we deserve; rather, according to his great love for us.

God, thank you for your compassion and mercy. You have forgiven me and you love me with abundance! Help me to dwell on this today.

Not Fearful

Such love has no fear, because perfect love expels all fear.
If we are afraid, it is for fear of punishment, and this shows
that we have not fully experienced his perfect love.

1 JOHN 4:18 NLT

Fear rears its ugly head in lots of ways: the spider waiting in your bathtub, the high bridge you pass going to your favorite park, the loud noise outside your bedroom window in the middle of the night. Fear can be gripping, paralyzing, or terrifying for some. For others, it is motivation to conquer weakness.

Jesus' followers had one such worry: what would happen on Judgment Day? Was Jesus' death enough to cover their sins completely and guarantee their eternity in heaven? John points out their fear as one of punishment. But there isn't room for fear alongside perfect love, and if we are abiding in the love of Jesus, then we have perfect love in us. Fear must surrender.

Jesus, I know I don't need to be fearful of anything because you overcame everything on the cross. I can rest easy in your perfect love, now and for all eternity.

Walking Confidently

Be my rock of refuge, to which I can always go;
give the command to save me,
for you are my rock and my fortress.
For you have been my hope, Sovereign LORD,
my confidence since my youth.

PSALM 71:3, 5 NIV

The foot traffic in the park was heavy: moms pushing strollers, joggers huffing over the trails, kids with baseball gloves and bats heading for open fields, couples meandering hand-in-hand under the leafy canopy. Observe closely and one can tell a lot about a person. Their posture, especially, is revealing. The man on the park bench, shoulders hunched, seems discouraged. One jogger lifts her head towards the sun, hopeful, while a mother's eyes dart nervously back and forth.

It is obvious when our hopes have sunk into shifting sand; we find no peace, no comfort, and no protective fortress from distress. Our foreheads wrinkle, our steps drift, our distraught hands clasp and wring. Our confidence is lost. What do you see when you look in the mirror? Worry lines or laugh lines? Are your eyes cloudy with anxieties or bright with possibilities? Are you hesitant or confident? God is the rock on which you can firmly plant your hopes.

Father, I lift my eyes to you today and walk with confidence.
You are the only hope and assurance I need.

Constant in Change

A furious squall came up, and the waves broke over the boat, so that it was nearly swamped. Jesus was in the stern, sleeping on a cushion. The disciples woke him and said to him, "Teacher, don't you care if we drown?" He got up, rebuked the wind and said to the waves, "Quiet! Be still!" Then the wind died down and it was completely calm. He said to his disciples, "Why are you so afraid? Do you still have no faith?"

MARK 4:37-40 NIV

It takes time to adjust to changing situations. Sailors need time to get their "sea legs," mountain climbers rest in order to adjust their lungs to altitude changes, and scuba divers surface slowly to regulate pressure. Even adjusting to daylight-savings can take some time.

During their time with Jesus, the disciples had to adjust quickly to radical situations. A daughter was raised from the dead, a boy's meager lunch multiplied, a demon was cast into a herd of pigs that threw themselves off a cliff. Could they have woken up in the morning and sufficiently prepared for such things? It seems as though the disciples never really adjusted to the unpredictability of life with Jesus. Have you?

Father God, no matter what changes I am facing, I can walk confidently when you are with me. You are prepared for everything; you are steady in the storm and you will not leave me to drown.

Finding Contentment

I have learned in whatever situation I am to be content.
I know how to be brought low, and I know how to abound.
In any and every circumstance, I have learned the secret of
facing plenty and hunger, abundance and need.

PHILIPPIANS 4:11-12 ESV

The key to unlocking contentment amidst the trials is in trusting that your needs have been met. Trust eliminates the spectrum between "life is good" and "life is bad." With trust, all life lived in the strength of Jesus is contentment. All life is satisfaction. Everything is a fulfillment of his promise that following him gives us just what we need.

Contentment grows in the midst of growing discomfort. Joy is found despite the trouble around every corner. A life of faith prospers amid the ruins. Comfort is found when you trust in your Father for everything. We don't need the trappings and the shimmer of the temporary. Whether we have everything or nothing, we trade it all for the eternal.

God, strengthen me to endure the worldly wanderings for the hope and promise of my eternal existence. I believe that you will meet my every need. I believe you for contentment today.

On the Right Path

Make me to know your ways, O LORD;
teach me your paths.
Good and upright is the LORD;
therefore he instructs sinners in the way.
He leads the humble in what is right,
and teaches the humble his way.
PSALM 25:4, 8-9 ESV

GPS has nothing on God. We use satellites because we want to know where we are going, how long it will take to get there, and how many miles we will travel on our journey. Our lives, however, don't have coordinates recognized by modern-day digital guides. Only our loving and faithful God leads us in the direction we really need to go. He *instructs sinners* who humbly learn to be *good and upright.*

The world's guidance can instruct you to take a left—directly into a murky pond. Satellites aren't as accurate as God's perfect instructions. By keeping his covenant and testimonies, we stay on the right path. With God, both the journey and the destination are worth the effort. When we keep his covenant and his testimonies, we receive the promises he gives us in his Word.

God, keep me on the right path. Thank you
for your faithfulness to me. When I wander,
you gently guide me back and restore me
to a right relationship with you.

Being Courageous

May he give you the power to accomplish all
the good things our faith prompts you to do.

2 THESSALONIANS 1:11 NLT

Courage is often associated with acts of bravery that defy typical human
experience: running through flames to save a child, jumping in a raging river
to pull someone to shore, or chasing down a thief to retrieve a stolen purse.
But courage doesn't always look so heroic. Courage is standing your ground
when you feel like running; it's saying yes to something you feel God is
telling you to do even when you aren't sure that you can do it.

Courage can be telling someone you don't want to hear their negative
thoughts about other people. It can be sharing your testimony with a room
full of people… or with one. Sometimes it takes courage just to leave
your house. When we place our trust and hope in God, he will give us the
courage we need to do the tasks he wants us to do. If that includes doing
something *heroic*, great! But let's not underestimate the importance of
walking courageously in the small things as well.

*Lord, so many things in life require me walking courageously.
Some small, and some heroic. Give me the courage I need to get
through each situation, so I can bring glory to your name.*

Depending On God

Be strong and courageous. Do not be afraid or terrified...for the LORD your God goes with you; he will never leave you nor forsake you.

DEUTERONOMY 31:6 NIV

Death and taxes. They say those are the two things we can depend on in life. Of course they don't mention the neighbor who fails to return the cordless drill (again), the empty fuel light blinking when you're late for work (again), and the spontaneous yet cheerful visitor ringing the doorbell when you're still in your pajamas at 3pm (again). Unpredictability is something else we can depend on!

Through every unpredictable situation, through all disappointments, delays, and disruptions, we can cling even more confidently to the faithfulness of God. He is the one solid rock on which we can firmly stand. He is steadfast and loyal, asking us to trust in his promises. God commands that we not be afraid or terrified; if it weren't possible, he wouldn't ask it of us. He guarantees that he will always be with us, no matter where we go. If it weren't true, he wouldn't promise it.

Thank you, Lord, that when life is unpredictable, I can still depend on you. You are always near me. Help me cling to you when everything else is shaking.

Stay the Course

Do you not know that in a race all the runners run, but only one gets the prize? Run in such a way as to get the prize. Everyone who competes in the games goes into strict training. They do it to get a crown that will not last, but we do it to get a crown that will last forever.

1 CORINTHIANS 9:24-25 NIV

Runners are human beings that have honed the evasive skill of self-control. They have the willpower to overcome physical pain and exhaustion. They have the stamina to push past throbbing muscles, breathlessness, and lead feet. They have the ability to follow through with the plan. So they do.

Running this race is the greatest challenge of your life. It requires self-control, motivation, and stamina. It requires submission to the training: saying yes every day to getting dressed, lacing up your shoes, and staying on the course. Determine to run the race so that you will win!

God, help me see life through your eyes. Let that motivate me to stay on course. Keep away the things which hinder me from putting my running shoes on and hitting the track.

Calm My Heart

When you go through deep waters and great trouble, I will be with you.
When you go through rivers of difficulty, you will not drown!
When you walk through the fire of oppression, you will not be burned up—
the flames will not consume you.

ISAIAH 43:2 TLB

When the hospital doors slide open and we aren't sure what news will greet us, God is compassionate. When the boss calls us for a meeting and dismissal is a real possibility, God is gentle. When we return home late at night to find our personal treasures stolen or destroyed, God is comforting. He cares so deeply for us.

Some see God as distant, vengeful, or condemning. Others see God as kind, affectionate, and attentive. Sometimes circumstances become too overwhelming. Mountains of anxiety rise up and we feel isolated and alone. Let no doubt take root; he is a God who cares deeply, loves fully, and remains faithful, ever at our side in times of trouble. Though our sorrows overwhelm us, he is the comfort that we need.

God, I choose to take your hand, offered in love, and receive
your comforting touch. I remember your faithfulness.
Let it calm my heart. You are with me,
and I will not drown or be consumed by fire.
I cling to your promises today.

My Confidence

"For my thoughts are not your thoughts,
neither are your ways my ways, declares the LORD.
For as the heavens are higher than the earth,
so are my ways higher than your ways
and my thoughts than your thoughts."

ISAIAH 55:8-9 ESV

In times of war, army strategists benefit from high vantage points. Looking upon the battlefield from above is the best way to formulate strategies for their troops. Before the use of satellite equipment and heat-sensing radar, views were limited to ground level, forcing strategists to use whatever maps and spies they could to predict enemy movement and position their men.

In the same way, our lives benefit from a higher viewpoint. When we rise above our circumstances and see life not from our own anxious, urgent, overwhelming perspective but from God's, life's battles become less intimidating as eternity's promises rise into view.

God, I know you have a plan for my life, but sometimes it is hard to see. Help me to confidently lift my head above the fray, and believe that you will lead me safely to victory.

Consolation

You, O LORD, are a shield about me,
My glory, and the One who lifts my head.
PSALM 3:3 NASB

Picture a young girl running a race. She leaps off to a great start when the gun sounds. She pushes her way to the front of the pack in no time and sets a pace that is tough to compete with. As she rounds the final corner with the finish line in sight, she stumbles. She tries desperately to regain her balance, but it's too late. She crashes to the ground. Trying to be brave, she jumps up and sprints the final yards to complete the race. Fourth place.

Head hung low, skinned knees burning, and vision blurry, she walks over to her coach. He gently lifts her chin to the sun, and brushes away the tears that have spilled over. As her bottom lip begins to quiver, he reassures her that everything is going to be ok. That life is full of painful moments that creep up unexpectedly, but it's also full of second chances. "Don't give up on yourself," he says, "I haven't given up on you."

God, when I've given up, run away, lost the plot, or stumbled and fallen, you don't give up on me. When I come to you with my head hung low, you lift my chin, look deep into my eyes, and whisper tender words of compassion that reach the deepest places in my heart. I am blessed.

DAY 123

Supernatural Courage

*I eagerly expect and hope that I will in no way be ashamed,
but will have sufficient courage so that now
as always Christ will be exalted in my body,
whether by life or by death.*

PHILIPPIANS 1:20 NIV

That's a pretty strong declaration: one exemplified in the life of Vibia Perpetua, a married noblewoman and Christian martyr who died at twenty-two years of age in Third Century Rome. Perpetua was arrested for her profession of faith in Christ and threatened with a harrowing execution if she did not renounce her faith. She had many compelling reasons to do just that—a nursing infant for one!

Early martyrdom wasn't only about dying for the profession of faith. It was about humiliation and torture carried out in a kind of sporting arena—with fans celebrating the demise of the victims. Yet, Perpetua displayed incredible fortitude in her final hour. Read her account and you'd have to agree that her courage could not possibly have been attributed to a human characteristic. Her courage came from God.

*Lord, having courage, being brave, remaining firm—
I can only hold on for so long. I call on your
supernatural strength to help me walk through
my trying circumstance. I know you hear me
and you will help me.*

DAY 124

My Deliverer

I waited patiently for the LORD;
he turned to me and heard my cry.
PSALM 40:1 NIV

God loves us with a sacrificial love that escapes our human understanding, overwhelms our human selfishness, and humbles our human pride. Through the sacrifice of his only Son, Jesus Christ, mankind is delivered from the fate of eternal separation from God.

When we are separated, bowed low and desperate, he hears our cry. When we are forgotten and despairing, he comforts our loneliness. And when, because of our own sin, we are wicked and depraved, he cleanses us of our offensiveness and makes us suitable for glory.

Thank you, Lord, for hearing me and coming to my rescue.
You have delivered me. You keep me steady and safe.
Let the song in my heart be a message to many today.

All Things Beautiful

He has made everything beautiful in its time.
He has also set eternity in the human heart; yet no one
can fathom what God has done from beginning to end.

ECCLESIASTES 3:11 NIV

We've probably all heard an older gentleman declare that his wife is more beautiful now than the day they married. And we likely thought, *He needs glasses.* What we fail to recognize in our outward-focused, airbrushed society, is that time really does make things beautiful. More accurately, time gives us better perspective on the true definition of beauty. Spending time with those we love affords us a glimpse into the depth of beauty that lies within. So while the external beauty may be fading, there is a wealth of beauty inside.

God's Word says that he makes all things beautiful in his time. *All* things. Whatever situation you are facing right now, it has the potential to create beauty in you. Perseverance, humility, grace, obedience—these are beautiful. But there's more. The beauty God creates in us cannot be fully described in human terms! There is eternal beauty to be found.

God, when I am met with challenges, I want to run to you and sit in your presence. When I dwell there, I reflect your character. Help me allow the difficulties in life to become a catalyst for true beauty.

Trusting the Rock

Through Christ you have come to trust in God.
And you have placed your faith and hope in God because
he raised Christ from the dead and gave him great glory.
1 PETER 1:21 NLT

Balancing at the edge of the cliff, a climber clutches the ropes. Far below, waves crash against the rocks, the spray reaching up toward her toes. She looks up at the guide, firmly gripping the rope, and then beyond his firm stance to the anchor hammered into the cliff side. With a firm push, her legs propel her beyond the ledge and out into space, dropping toward the sea.

Of course she trusts the guide. His strong grip, years of experience, skill, and familiarity with the landscape go a long way in convincing her that she will belay safely to the bottom of the cliff. But it's the rock, pierced by the anchor, which gains her deepest faith. The rock will not fail, will not crumble, and will never falter under her weight.

God, I trust you. As I leap, sometimes stumbling, along the cliffs of life, you are my anchor and my only hope. I can jump with ease from any height, knowing that your strong arms of love will surround me. My destiny is sure.

Unmatched Faithfulness

Your lovingkindness, O LORD, extends to the heavens,
Your faithfulness reaches to the skies.
PSALM 36:5 NASB

Few love stories demonstrate a higher level of faithfulness than that depicted by the life of Hosea the prophet. He was given what seemed to be a very unfair task—to take a prostitute as a wife and commit to loving her. He would watch as his wife and the mother of his children chose to leave the family and return to her life of prostitution. But it didn't end there. Hosea went in search of his wife, and finding her in her debauchery, he *paid* to bring her back home with him—guilty, broken, and dirty. It would seem a romantic tale of undying love had it happened naturally. However, this story is even more inconceivable when considering that Hosea walked into it knowing what would happen.

It sounds oddly familiar, doesn't it? Jesus, commissioned by the Father, pursued us until we decided to become *his*. But we just can't seem to keep ourselves out of the mess of this world. Jesus doesn't quit. He comes for us again. The price he paid to restore our relationship was his life. He gave up everything to bring us home. That is faithfulness in its fullest measure.

God, help me not to measure your faithfulness by
my lack of it. Yours cannot be exhausted.
I choose to believe that you continue to
love me in spite of my failures.

Temper Tantrums

What is causing the quarrels and fights among you? Don't they come from the evil desires at war within you? You want what you don't have, so you scheme and kill to get it. You are jealous of what others have, but you can't get it, so you fight and wage war to take it away from them.

JAMES 4:1-2 NLT

Temper tantrums are as common for adults as they are for children; they just look different in action. Children haven't learned to curb the screaming and stomping vent of frustration or anger, while adults have more restrained behavior. But the heart is the same, and the reactions stem from the same provocation.

James cuts right to the heart of sin. We want what we want but we don't have it, so we throw a tantrum. It's amazing how simple it is! Watch a child and this truth will play out soon enough. Watch an adult, and it may be more difficult to discern, but unfortunately it is there in all of us. Thank God for his endless supply of grace!

I praise you, God, for your amazing grace,
which is extended to me in the midst of my tantrums.
I draw near to you for your cleansing and purifying grace.
Wash over me today.

My Freedom

Creation itself will be set free from its bondage to corruption
and obtain the freedom of the glory of the children of God.

ROMANS 8:21 ESV

Some days begin with praises on our lips and a song to God in our hearts.
Humility covers us like a velvet cloth, soothing and delicate and gentle. The truth
of God plays on repeat: "God is good! God is good! I am free!" and the entire
world's darkness cannot interrupt the chorus. But other days begin by fumbling
with the snooze button and forfeiting the chance to meet him in the quiet
stillness. Pride, then, is a sneaky companion, pushing and bitter and ugly, and we
wonder if we will ever delight with God again. We feel bound.

The ups and downs should be familiar by now, perhaps, but can we ever
become accustomed to the holy living side-by-side with our flesh? One glorious
day, flesh will give way to freedom, and there will be no side-by-side. Only
the holy will remain. This leaves praise on our lips and a song in our hearts,
the unending chorus of his goodness, the velvet covering as we sit before his
heavenly throne.

God, I know you want me to rest in your presence.
You are faithful and tender. When I spend time with you,
there's no need to hide. I can be exactly who I am
and say what I need to say. Thank you.

Perfect Friend

"Here I am! I stand at the door and knock. If anyone hears my voice and opens the door, I will come in and eat with that person, and they with me."
REVELATION 3:20 NIV

God created you for relationship with him just as he created Adam and Eve. He delights in your voice, your laughter, and your ideas. He longs to fellowship with you. When life gets difficult, do you run to him with your frustrations? When you're overwhelmed with sadness or grief, do you carry your pain to him? In the heat of anger or frustration, do you call on him for freedom? He is a friend that offers all of this to us—and more—in mercy and love. He is worthy of our friendship.

The friendship he offers to us is a gift of immeasurable worth. There is no one like him; indeed, there is none as worthy of our fellowship than God Almighty, our Maker and Redeemer. Train your heart to run first to God with your pain, joy, frustration, and excitement. His friendship will never let you down!

God, you are the perfect friend. If I think of all I need in a friendship, I know that I can find it in you. Thank you that your friendship surpasses all of my expectations.

He Gives Me Grace

He gives more grace. Therefore He says:
"God resists the proud,
But gives grace to the humble."

JAMES 4:6 NKJV

Maybe you've heard stories of people suffering tragedy, or maybe you're living through a tragedy yourself. Either way, if you had been told you would encounter tragedy, you'd probably have thought, *There's no possible way I could go through that.* And you would be right. You couldn't. Why? Because you haven't yet been given the grace to walk through it yet.

Do we really believe that people who go through tragedy and come out stronger on the other side are any different than ourselves? That they are superhuman somehow? They aren't. They just got to a place where they recognized their desperate need for God's grace in their circumstance—and they asked him for it.

Thank you, Lord, that you don't call me to walk through seasons of difficulty on my own. You give me as much grace as I need for every situation. Help me to be humble enough to admit that I need your help, that I can't walk through hardship on my own.

DAY 132

My Guide

All the paths of the Lord are steadfast
love and faithfulness,
for those who keep his covenant
and his testimonies.

PSALM 25:10 ESV

There is a Family Circus cartoon where the son is asked to take out the garbage. The drawing then traces the tangled and erratic pathway between the boy and his final destination. He bounces over couches, through windows, under wheelbarrows, around trees, between siblings, all on the way to the curbside trash can.

Our lives can feel like this at times: unpredictable, illogical, and inconsistent. Changes in work, marriage, family, or church can make the road seem irrational, uneven, and confusing. But God makes us the promise of a steadfast path when we keep his covenant. When we consider our lives through our limited human perspective, the path seems wavering. But the guidance of Jesus Christ is, in fact, steadfast!

God, you have chosen my path and set my feet upon it. I know it is a path of love and faithfulness. I trust you even in the refinement of my path. Though it might be uncomfortable at times, I still trust you because you are perfect and you are good.

Healer

"Daughter, your faith has made you well; go in peace
and be healed of your affliction."

MARK 5:34 NASB

The woman in the crowd had suffered for more than a decade. All of her
money had been spent on doctors, but instead of finding healing she was
worse than ever. She had one hope, and she reached for it as Jesus passed
by her in the crowd. She believed that just a touch, not even from his holy
hand but from his garment alone, would bring the healing she desired.
In his brief but blessed response, we hear Jesus' heart for his ailing child:
*Daughter, I love your faith! You came to the right place for healing; I know
everything about you and the pain you have suffered. Because you have
believed in my love for you, you are healed! Be at peace.*

Often, we become fixated on doctoring our own wounds so we can make
it through the day. They may be physical, emotional, mental, or spiritual
and we may have tried every possible means to treat them. Why not turn
instead to the one who can fully repair us?

**Father, you know my burdens. I believe that you are good, and you
can heal me. I put my faith in you and ask you to make me whole.**

He Is My Hope

There is surely a future hope for you,
and your hope will not be cut off.

PROVERBS 23:18 NIV

Abraham took God at his word. Everything about his present circumstance made the idea that he would have a son ridiculous. His body was as good as dead. His own wife laughed at the thought that she, a woman of ninety, body worn out and barren, would nurse a child of her own. And yet, God had said it—this God that could give life even to the dead and who could call into existence things that didn't yet exist.

Hope starts with the promises of God. When doubt, discouragement, or despair threatens your soul, take heart. We have a God that has already spoken words of life and certainty that will prove to both revive and carry us. Hope is taking God at his Word, believing that all he has said is sure.

God, you are my trustworthy anchor. I confidently expect that you will do all you have said you will do—even the things that seem impossible. I choose to believe you for the fulfillment of your promises.

My Inspiration

The precepts of the LORD are right,
giving joy to the heart.
The commands of the LORD are radiant,
giving light to the eyes.

PSALM 19:8 NIV

Children often wonder about the face of God, imagining what he looks like and how his voice might sound. *I want to see God! Where is he?* Where, indeed, beloved? God is in the beauty, showing off for you. When you see something lovely, you are seeing your Daddy's handiwork. When you hold a newborn baby, and look up and marvel, "I see God!" truly, God is there.

It's an amazing circle, this inspiration. He gives us so many good gifts—vibrant colors, bursting flavors, comforting warmth, moving melodies, and unimaginable beauty—that our hearts cannot help but respond. And our inspirations pour out in a beautiful offering of worship back to our Creator. Even his commands, his laws, and his guidance are inspiring! Described as right and radiant, his acts of loving and devoted instructions keep us safe. They also draw us nearer to our Father and give joy and light.

*God, I prayerfully submit to your leadership and
the lovely gifts you have planned for me. You are my inspiration.
I see you in the beauty all around me!*

He Knows Me by Name

Lord, you know everything there is to know about me.
You've examined my innermost being
With your loving gaze.
You perceive every movement of my heart and soul,
And understand my every thought
Before it even enters my mind.
You are so intimately aware of me, Lord,
You read my heart like an open book
And you know all the words I'm about to speak
Before I even start a sentence!
You know every step I will take,
Before my journey even begins!

PSALM 139:1-4 TPT

There are people who are terrible with names. And then there are parents. They address you by every name in the household—quite possibly including the dog—all while looking you in the eye… and they gave you the name in the first place!

There may be thousands of people with *your* name, or there might just be a handful. Either way, it makes no difference to God. He doesn't take a stab in the dark when you are approaching him, guessing a name and hoping he gets it right. He knows exactly who you are and why you are coming to him. He knows why you've stayed away for so long. He knows your deepest need, your most painful wound, and your darkest thoughts. And still he loves you.

Father God, you really do know me. And in knowing me,
you still love me. Thank you for your heart toward me.

My Joy

Be truly glad. There is wonderful joy ahead. You love him even though you have never seen him. Though you do not see him now, you trust him; and you rejoice with a glorious, inexpressible joy.

1 PETER 1:6, 8 NLT

Life is full of pain and sorrow. Jesus, described as a man of sorrows and acquainted with grief, was no stranger to mourning, weeping, and at one point even declared in agony that he was sorrowful unto death. Jeremiah cried out that his heart was sick within him and his sadness could not be healed. Paul carried burdens so far beyond his strength that he despaired of life. David's pain groans off the pages of the psalms, and Job went so far as to say he wished he had died at birth.

Can joy be found within the piercing anguish of loss? The purest form of joy is often experienced in the arms of sorrow. Joy flows in the middle of the darkness as we trust in God's perfect ways. Joy is clinging to our Savior with the knowledge that Jesus is still who he says he is, even when our pain feels overwhelming. Joy is going to the cross of Christ to sustain us, to give us hope, and to receive his grace and mercy for the days ahead.

God, help me to experience joy in the midst of walking through my difficulty. I know that you are with me and you are holding me.

God Is Just

He did not retaliate when he was insulted,
nor threaten revenge when he suffered.
He left his case in the hands of God,
who always judges fairly.

1 PETER 2:23 NLT

Our parents were right: life's not fair. We probably learned that first when we didn't get the larger half of the cookie, or when one of our siblings got to go somewhere special while we were at school. As we got older, we might have learned about the lack of fairness a little more harshly: perhaps through wrongful accusations, denied promotions, or unmet expectations.

It's easy to be disappointed with the unfairness of life. When wrongfully accused or misunderstood, it's hard not to take it to heart. We either want to defend our reputation until the bitter end, or disappear. When faced with these situations, we can rest in the knowledge that God is just. He will judge everyone fairly.

Thank you, God, that I don't have to worry about my accusers fighting their case more convincingly. I don't leave my judgment in the hands of a jury, and even the best attorney can't make a case against me that will last into eternity. You know my situation God, and, more importantly, you know my heart.

DAY 139

His Kindness

The LORD directs the steps of the godly.
He delights in every detail of their lives.
Though they stumble, they will never fall,
for the LORD holds them by the hand.

PSALM 37:23-24 NLT

Holding hands is a beautiful act when done in love. We might hold hands with a child to cross the street, to help an aging stranger off of the bus, or to embrace even the smallest part of our beloved while strolling through the park. We grasp hands for a moment, and give safety, kindness, or affection through the simple act.

Can you imagine that God's hand in this same act is extended to those who put their faith in him? Surely his sons and daughters need the spiritual comfort, guidance, and fellowship of God's hand more than any other. And we can be certain that God delights in extending his hand to us as well.

Father, I take comfort in your kindness. You lead me rightly.
I cannot fall when I follow your lead because your
loving grip will never let me go.

He Is Love

We love because he first loved us. If anyone says,
"I love God," and hates his brother, he is a liar;
for he who does not love his brother whom he has
seen cannot love God whom he has not seen.

1 JOHN 4:19-20 ESV

God's greatest commandments are to love him and to love one another.
Loving him may come easy; after all, he is patient and loving himself.
But the second part of his command can be difficult because it means
loving intrusive neighbors at the backyard barbecue, offensive cousins
at Christmas dinner, rude cashiers at the grocery store check-out, and
insufferable guests who have stayed one night too many in the guestroom.

Loving one another is only possible when we love like God. When we love
out of our humanity, sin gets in the way. Obeying the command to love
begins with God's love. When we realize how great his love is for us—how
undeserved, unending, and unconditional—
we are humbled because we didn't earn it.

*Lord, help me represent you to the world.
I know it's not easy, but I want to follow your
example and love as you did. Give me the grace
and strength I need to carry this out.*

He Is All I Need

Happy are those
who do not follow the advice of the wicked,
or take the path that sinners tread,
or sit in the seat of scoffers;
but their delight is in the law of the LORD,
and on his law they meditate day and night.
They are like trees
planted by streams of water,
which yield their fruit in its season,
and their leaves do not wither.
In all that they do, they prosper.

PSALM 1:1-3 NRSV

Thanks to a modern diet of technology and social media, women today can feast on heaping portions of gossip, envy, boastful pride, and selfishness. It is not a nourishing diet, but it is deviously sweet.

Praise God for his nourishment! His Word is as relevant for us today as it was for David thousands of years ago. Meditate on these words, and hear his voice calling to you. When we spend time with him and read his Word, he is the path to joy and delight. Under his nourishment we yield delicious fruit without the threat of withering. We prosper!

God, I admit that at times I am underfed on your Word.
I'm malnourished from overeating at the modern-day buffet of social
media and entertainment. Help me get rid of these unhealthy habits
and embrace you more fully each day.

My Peace

"The Advocate, the Holy Spirit, whom the Father will send in my name, will teach you all things and will remind you of everything I have said to you. Peace I leave with you; my peace I give you. I do not give to you as the world gives. Do not let your hearts be troubled and do not be afraid."

JOHN 14:26-27 NIV

Peace is much-desired but often elusive. Just when we seem to be getting life under control, a new disaster strikes. Just when we find enough calm to settle our minds, a bigger calamity arises. Or worse, the waves of difficulty come one after another with no end in sight. Will there ever be an end to our conflicts? Why does peace elude us?

We find everything we need when we look to God's Word. The peace begged for on bumper stickers will always elude the world; the peace of Jesus Christ is the only lasting peace that we can attain while walking this earth. Because he knew our weak flesh, Jesus promised us a path to his peace even in this world of struggle—our Advocate, the Holy Spirit.

Jesus, I need your peace. When my heart is troubled and afraid, only you can give me the peace I truly need—the peace you promised to us so long ago, knowing we would need it.

Retirement

Let us throw off everything that hinders and the sin that so easily entangles.
And let us run with perseverance the race marked out for us, fixing our eyes
on Jesus… so that you will not grow weary and lose heart.

HEBREWS 12:1-3 NIV

There is no such thing as "retirement" for those who serve God. There won't
be a spiritual pension waiting for us so that we can finally relax and let others
finish God's good work. We might have travel ideas, plans to focus on a
hobby, or dreams of unwinding and living easy while everyone else labors
away, but God doesn't stop using us!

Our prayers, testimonies, encouragement, wisdom, and faith must never
retire from use. Bringing glory to the kingdom of God is a full-time effort
requiring long-term endurance. While we wait to enjoy that glory, God has
plans that aren't put off by our aging bodies. We are encouraged to continue
on without interruption. We are promised those beautiful words of approval,
"Well done, good and faithful servant!" upon the completion of our earthly
journey.

*God, I believe in my heart that this journey will be worth it in the
end. I know I need to slow down and refuel, and I know I will make
mistakes. But I will keep my eyes fixed on you. Even if I only make it a
few inches forward each day, I will keep moving ahead.
I do not want to grow weary and lose heart.*

He Hears My Prayers

Why am I praying like this? Because I know you will answer me,
O God! Yes, listen as I pray.

PSALM 17:6 TLB

There are those days when words fail us. We can barely string a coherent
sentence together, let alone articulate exactly what we need. Grief has
found us and it seems to have taken over our ability to think, or speak,
or pray. Tears roll silently down our cheeks, our hearts ache, and still no
words come.

Be encouraged. Not only does God hear your prayers when they tumble
clumsily from your lips, he knows what you need prior to you asking. He's
aware of what you require to get through today before you can put it into
words. And when you do finally put words to your thoughts that seem
completely inadequate? It doesn't matter. God heard your heart.

Thank you, God, that you interpret my words through my heart.
My message to you is not lost in translation. I believe that
you hear me when I call out to you, and you will answer me.

Provision

Because of our faith, Christ has brought us into this place of
undeserved privilege where we now stand, and we confidently
and joyfully look forward to sharing God's glory.

ROMANS 5:2 NLT

Pull up to the drive-through, place an order for the coffee that will help
start the day, and hear the cashier's words, "Your order was paid for by the
car in front of you." This unexpected generosity gives birth to humbling
gratitude, and the day is now overcome with God's presence. A stranger
may have been the instrument of kind provision, but the inspiration is
unmistakable.

God is the author of generosity, providing us with all we need. Look at all he
gave to Adam and Eve, and how little he asked for in return! They walked in
his presence daily, enjoying authentic relationship with their Father. Even
when they ate what they knew they shouldn't, God provided atonement
for them.

*God, I know I have sinned and deserve death. Thank you for Christ,
my substantial provision! You bless me each and every day,
whether I acknowledge it or not. You work your love out for me
in generous portions! I am so grateful for your generosity.*

DAY 146

Clean Again

Teach me your ways, O LORD,
that I may live according to your truth!
Grant me purity of heart,
so that I may honor you.

PSALM 86:11 NLT

If you've ever tried to clean a white dog who had decided to run around in the mud, you'll know it seems like an impossible task to get rid of every speck of dirt—especially if said puppy isn't too keen on the bathing procedure. If it could just sit and allow its owner to work carefully and methodically, all traces of dirt could likely be eliminated. But often neither the dog nor its owner has that kind of patience.

Cleaning up the sin in our lives can feel similar. Finding and ridding ourselves of all impurity can be a slow and painful process. It might seem downright impossible at times. Maybe we don't want to be examined, or perhaps sitting still is the problem. The good news is we don't have to try to purify ourselves. We allow God to do it for us. Fortunately, he is patient, and he has the perfect solution. He uses the sacrifice of his Son to wash away all of our dirt. Every last speck.

Lord, I trust you to gently wash away all of my filth. Make me pure again. Help me to sit still for long enough to let you do your redemptive work in my heart.

Purpose in Your Heart

The purpose in a man's heart is like deep water,
but a man of understanding will draw it out.

PROVERBS 20:5 ESV

God has placed a purpose in every single one of us. We are all meant to play a beautiful and important role in his eternal kingdom. We've each been blessed with the skills and passion to fulfill God's purposes both here on earth and in his kingdom forever.

Life and circumstance can disguise our purpose. We can get caught up in the daily grind and forget to focus in on the eternal vision he's breathed into us. We must make it our goal to unearth our unique purposes for which we were specifically created. When we understand this purpose is when we will truly begin to live fully alive as we were intended to.

God, keep me always seeking to fulfill your plan for my life. Don't let me lose sight of your vision for me. I want to accomplish your purposes and I want to be available to be used by you in whatever way you desire.

DAY 148

Refreshed in His Presence

Repent and return, so that your sins may be wiped away, in order that times of refreshing may come from the presence of the Lord.

ACTS 3:19 NASB

Sin is exhausting. It kills us from the inside out. We cannot live an abundant life in Christ while still pursuing a life of sin. The beauty about salvation and the grace of our God is that all we have to do is return to him in repentance and our sin will be erased.

As we walk away from our sin and return to God, we find refreshment and restoration. We will be given grace to walk forward in forgiveness, and be clothed with power to continue in a life of righteousness and strength to resist future temptations. His blood will cleanse us, his grace will renew us, his power will restore us, and his presence will refresh us.

Heavenly Father, search my heart and convict me of any sin that is causing weariness in my spirit. Cleanse and erase the sin from my life. Bring your refreshing to my soul so I can live the grace-filled life that you desire for me. Thank you for your cleansing and for your love.

Reverse Gossip

Gracious words are like a honeycomb,
sweetness to the soul and health to the body.
PROVERBS 16:24 ESV

We know that our words are powerful. We understand that with what we say we can build someone up or tear them down. But apart from the words we speak directly to one another, we must realize that even the words we speak behind someone's back can have a tremendous effect on them.

From celebrity gossip, to telling our friends about an experience we had with someone, we talk about others all the time. These conversations tend to be negative. What if we decided to be radically set apart with our words and conversations? What if we began a movement to reverse gossip by spreading word of the greatness in people instead? What if we spent our time dreaming about how we could help others instead of bettering ourselves? Our hearts and our lives would reflect Jesus much more clearly if we would simply change the way we speak about others.

*Lord Jesus, help me to tame my tongue. Give me
the gift of gracious words. Let kindness flow easily
from my lips and let me speak greatness over others
on a daily basis. I want to bring sweetness to
the souls of those you've placed in my life.*

Righteousness Poured Out

Sow righteousness for yourselves,
reap the fruit of unfailing love,
and break up your unplowed ground;
for it is time to seek the LORD,
until he comes
and showers his righteousness on you.

HOSEA 10:12 NIV

A day will come when we see our Savior face-to-face. We will dwell in the light of his presence for eternity. But for right now, here on this earth, we are in a season of seeking him and of preparing our hearts for his coming glory.

When we plant righteousness in our lives, we will reap the harvest of the unfailing love of Christ. We open the door to every one of the blessings he has for us when we simply open our hearts to him. And we cannot plant righteousness if there is any ground in our hearts that isn't soft and ready. By daily coming before him, bowing our knee, examining our hearts, and allowing him to water our souls with his Word, we will be softened by his love.

God, I need your presence so desperately in my life. I thank you that I can stand in your presence here and now. Soften any hard ground in my heart so that I can be ready to receive all that you have for me.

She Who Has Believed

"Blessed is she who has believed that the Lord
would fulfill his promises to her!"

LUKE 1:45 NIV

Promise is often what keeps us going. We need something to look forward to—a banner to hold up and a finish line to run toward. When we begin to lose faith that we will reach that finish line, or when we start to doubt that the dream will ever come true, that is when we falter and begin to lose our way.

There is so much power in our belief. Think about those in Scripture to whom Jesus said, "Your faith has made you well." God has always rewarded a believing heart. He is glorified in the faith of his children and in their trust in his promises. Don't lose sight of what he has promised you. Believe that he will fulfill it no matter how unlikely it seems to you. He will not forget you. And he will bless you for your unwavering faith in him.

God, help me to always believe that you will bring to pass the dreams you've given me. I desire your blessing, and I want to be known as one who never lost faith in your promise.

Something New

"In the same way I will not cause pain without allowing something new to be born," says the LORD. "If I cause you the pain, I will not stop you from giving birth to your new nation," says your God.

ISAIAH 66:9 NCV

God never causes pain without purpose. He doesn't allow us to weather a season of loss and destruction in our lives without preparing a place of peaceful restoration on the other side.

If you are enduring a season of struggle, hold on to the promise that something new is being born out of your trial. And no matter how painful the process, or how much you feel like there's no way anything could be worth this difficulty, know that your heavenly Father sees everything you're going through and he will bring you new birth.

Thank you, Jesus, that you see my pain. Thank you that you promise not to allow pain without something new being born in my life. You are a God who restores, re-creates, and establishes his people. Help me to trust you even in my seasons of pain.

He Restores My Soul

"Stop wailing," Jesus said. "She is not dead but asleep." They laughed at
him, knowing that she was dead. But he took her by the hand and said,
"My child, get up!" Her spirit returned, and at once she stood up.
Then Jesus told them to give her something to eat.

LUKE 8:52-55 NIV

Do you know whose you are? Your father and mother rightly claim you as
their child, but do you recognize Jesus as the one who restores you as his?
He knows your coming and going, your every inner working; you are his.

How difficult it is to put our needs into the hands of the Father! Do we
dare hope? Imagine watching your child die and feeling the despair of her
absence, only to have Jesus claim that she is asleep. Both the girl's father
and Jesus loved the child; both claimed her as their daughter. But only
Jesus commanded her spirit and her life. His child hears his voice and obeys
his command; she gets up and is restored!

God, you are faithful to the deepest needs of my heart;
you know me full well! I listen today for your voice and
ask for my spirit to be renewed.

Break Every Chain

His purpose in all of this is that they should seek after God,
and perhaps feel their way toward him and find him—
though he is not far from any one of us.

ACTS 17:27 TLB

There is a chance to start over—every day if we need to. From the inside out, we can be transformed and our hearts renewed. We can essentially remake ourselves with the help, healing, and transformative nature of Christ! Jesus died on the cross to promise us a life free from the bondage of sin, free from hopelessness, free from any chains that try to trap us. In Christ, we are set free.

We need to hear the truth of Christ's promise for us and stop the cycle of hopelessness, defeat, and bondage to sin. All we need to do is get on our knees and pray.

Father God, I ask for your voice to permeate the deepest,
saddest part of me. I know you want to take care of me.
Thank you for continuing to pursue my heart.

The King

So that we would know for sure that we are his true children, God released the Spirit of Sonship into our hearts—moving us to cry out intimately, "My Father! You're our true Father!" Now we're no longer living like slaves under the law, but we enjoy being God's very own sons and daughters! And because we're his, we can access everything our Father has.

GALATIANS 4:6-7 TPT

Picture a beautiful white castle perched on a mountain top overlooking a crystal-clear lake surrounded by trees. Decadent turrets and towers reach high into the sky, affording a breathtaking view. High walls, a watchtower, and open parapets ensure maximum protection from enemy forces. Inside, vaulted ceilings and crystal chandeliers tower above sprawling staircases. Ornate sculptures and paintings grace the walls, and the grand hall echoes with laughter.

The King appears. For a moment, you tremble, unsure of how to respond. Then, as he advances toward you with arms wide open, you remember. *This is my Daddy. And this is my home.* You run as fast as you can into those arms, and lose yourself in his warm embrace.

It sounds like a fairytale, but that picture doesn't even do justice to the home or the Father awaiting us. Gold, silver, sparkling jewels, decadence, opulence, splendor, immeasurable love, joy, peace, and unbroken relationship—it's our inheritance! The King of all kings calls us his children. That means we are royalty, and everything he has he wants to share with us.

Father, thank you for the inheritance I have as your child. This life has plenty of trouble and suffering, but the promise of eternity with you, my majestic King, is more than worth it!

Hiding Place

Wherever I am, though far away at the ends of the earth, I will cry to you for help. When my heart is faint and overwhelmed, lead me to the mighty, towering Rock of safety. For you are my refuge, a high tower where my enemies can never reach me.

PSALM 61:2-3 TLB

When emotional injuries that were buried long ago come to the surface of life, they transform from past scars to raw, gaping wounds, brand new and scorching. Earthly bandages cannot completely heal the pain. We need God's touch, the balm of his tenderness, upon us. It aches, but he is a safe hiding place—a refuge when we are afraid to walk through the pain.

Abiding in his safety and leaving the wound open is the hardest part. We have to see it, feel it, and let God walk us through the healing process. And that might take time. But he is a loving, worthy, compassionate Father, whose treatment roots out all infection and disease so that the scars can remain healed. We are safe when we are in his care, and he promises to protect us.

Lord, I believe that I am precious to you. You are fiercely protective, eternally faithful, and your love is inescapable. I bring you all of my hurt, pain, regret, and brokenness so you can heal me and put me back together. I take refuge in your arms today.

He Satisfies Me

O my dove, in the clefts of the rock,
in the crannies of the cliff,
let me see your face,
let me hear your voice,
for your voice is sweet,
and your face is lovely.

SONG OF SOLOMON 2:14 ESV

Stress threatens to get the better of us, and sometimes we just want to hide. Remembering that secret bar of chocolate in the pantry, we may scurry off to do just that: bury ourselves away with the temporary but sweet comfort that helps the world slow down,
if only for a moment.

The same instinct can arise with God. We get overwhelmed by his ministry or overdue for his forgiveness or out of touch with his Word and lose track of who he is. Instead of running toward him, we hide from him and look for other ways to meet our needs. We cannot hide from him, and in love he calls out to us.

God, I cannot outrun your love for me and I don't want to try.
I choose to leave the false safety of the clefts and crannies and
pantries with hidden chocolate to feel the pleasure of your friendship.

Security Blanket

In peace I will lie down and sleep,
for you alone, LORD,
make me dwell in safety.

PSALM 4:8 NIV

Have you ever spent hours—or minutes that seemed like hours—searching frantically for Blankie, Paci, or Lambie in an attempt to quiet the inconsolable child sprawled on the floor? Ah, that wonderful security item. The magic silencer. The instant peace maker. As kids grow older, we try to wean them off those security items: the blankets that are torn to shreds, the teddy bears with missing eyes, or the pacifiers that are chewed beyond recognition. Most children don't agree that they could do without the security of those things—and they have a point.

Think of all the times you've walked through trials and found yourself at a loss. Where do you go to feel secure? The best place you can go is to God. He is our security, and he gives us the strength we need to press on. We should feel lost when we don't have him nearby. When he's right beside us—sharing our pillow in the dark of night, riding beside us in the car, or sitting next to us at our desk—we sense that everything is going to be ok.

Lord God, I look solely to you for my security.
There is no better place to find it.

Always In Control

Do not be anxious about anything, but in every situation, by prayer and petition, with thanksgiving, present your requests to God. And the peace of God, which transcends all understanding, will guard your hearts and your minds in Christ Jesus.

PHILIPPIANS 4:6-7 NIV

The counselor's suggestion box overflowed with ideas from the school's young students, varying from inventive and reasonable (replacing fluorescent lights with tons of twinkling Christmas lights) to imaginative but impractical (covering the hallways with giant slip n' slides). But each one was read aloud during weekly staff meetings. The children's ideas never decreased in volume or zeal; they believed that their school could be greater than any other, and that their school counselor not only respected but valued their input.

As a result, students also approached the counselor with their personal troubles; he heard about failures on the soccer field, fights with best friends, botched geometry quizzes, and sibling rivalries. His door was always open, and the seats weren't empty for long. What did he offer these young hearts and minds? What was the secret to giving them serenity in the midst of those tumultuous years? He mimicked the example set by God, our great Counselor, who hears our worries and protects us with his peace.

Father, you are my tried-and-true method: you bend your ear to my anxieties, my longings, my frustrations, and my worship. Thank you for valuing my petitions. I want to be more like you.

Blood, Sweat, and Tears

"I will sing to the LORD, for he has triumphed gloriously;
the horse and his rider he has thrown into the sea.
The LORD is my strength and my song,
and he has become my salvation;
this is my God, and I will praise him,
my father's God, and I will exalt him."

EXODUS 15:1-2 ESV

Have you ever watched the Olympics and marveled at the incredible strength, discipline, and God-given talent of the athletes? Watching interviews, we commonly hear the question, "Where do you get the strength—the motivation?" Daily life, while not an Olympic sport, requires its own motivation if we are to push through the blood, sweat, and tears to the gold medal that awaits us. Moses, after the victorious escape from Pharaoh's army, praises the source of their strength in the Scripture above.

Are you facing an Olympic-sized trial? Are you wondering where your strength to endure will come from? Does it seem absolutely crazy that God can and will lift you up to overcome? Remember that he is your strength and your song; trust his power to be yours and praise him because he is worthy.

Lord, you alone have the strength I need to make it through this struggle. You support me time and time again. I trust you, thank you, and exalt you.

The Right Foundation

Let your roots grow down into him, and let your lives
be built on him. Then your faith will grow strong in
the truth you were taught, and you will overflow
with thankfulness.

COLOSSIANS 2:7 NLT

His brothers laughed at his heavy laboring, day in and day out, while they
lounged around. Their homes had taken no time at all to complete, and they
liked them just fine. Until the wolf came, with his gusting huffs and puffs
and then... The story is as familiar as its lesson: take the time to do things
right so when trouble comes you will be safe. Build with worthy materials,
and you'll have something that lasts through the fiercest of storms.

God is the rock on which we can build with confidence. Not only can we
have assurance in his firm foundation, but he promises to bless us as we
dwell with him. Rains, flooding, gusting wind will come, but he will see us
through every storm with truth which will strengthen our faith. We will see
him triumph over sin and darkness, and we will overflow with thankfulness!

God, help me to rejoice in the midst of the storms. As the winds howl
around me, let my faith grow strong. Nothing can come against me
that will blow my house down when I'm on your strong foundation.

Supported

Whom have I in heaven but you?
And earth has nothing I desire besides you.
My flesh and my heart may fail,
but God is the strength of my heart
and my portion forever.

PSALM 73:25-26 NIV

When considering a home remodeling project, it's important to determine where the support beams are. If we just knock a wall down here and there to create more space, it could have a detrimental effect on the rest of the structure. Whether a building topples because of faulty construction, a bad foundation, or extraordinary loads, you can bet the support beams were compromised.

Support beams can be like those people in our lives that we look up to. People we love. People we respect. People we depend on. Sometimes they fall—and we might not realize we were leaning on them until they do. When they go down, it can be hard to recover. They might leave a wake of destruction in their collapse. The only support beam you can lean on and guarantee it will never shake, bend, or crumble under pressure is God.

*Father, when the world around me seems to have collapsed,
and I find myself floundering around looking for something firm
to take hold of, I choose to grab your hand.
You are steady and sure, and your love is safe.*

My All in All

I fall to my knees and pray to the Father, the Creator of everything in heaven and on earth. I pray that from his glorious, unlimited resources he will empower you with inner strength through his Spirit. Then Christ will make his home in your hearts as you trust in him. Your roots will grow down into God's love and keep you strong. And may you have the power to understand, as all God's people should, how wide, how long, how high, and how deep his love is. May you experience the love of Christ, though it is too great to understand fully. Then you will be made complete with all the fullness of life and power that comes from God.

EPHESIANS 3:14-19 NLT

Gloomy days happen. In the midst of the dreariness it helps to hear the voice of a friend, especially one who points us so perfectly to the sustenance we need. The prayer of Paul, addressed to those in desperate need of hearing the promises of life in Jesus Christ, is a prayer for you.

Pray this for yourself, your friend, your neighbor, your coworker. Pray until you feel the roots deepening and strengthening in love. Pray it again and again until the power to understand overwhelms you—he is all you need! Pray it until the fullness of God's love for you overcomes your gloom.

God, I will hold on to this prayer until your life and power break through the clouds and shine brightly on my face. You are all I need. I can trust you for everything!

Comfortable

Blessed be the God and Father of our Lord Jesus Christ, the Father of mercies and God of all comfort, who comforts us in all our tribulation.

2 CORINTHIANS 1:3 NKJV

We have all experienced loss in our lives—some to a greater degree than others. In these times when we are grieving the loss of a loved one, a job, or even experiencing the loss of a relationship breakdown, it is good to acknowledge that pain is uncomfortable. We cannot hide from feeling angry, disappointed, extremely sad, or lonely. However, we can bring these emotions to our heavenly Father, and ask him to ease the pain.

The Scriptures say that Jesus is the Father of mercies and is able to comfort us in all our troubles. He can bring peace, joy, and the comfort of knowing his presence each and every day. He can bring help from others. His Word can bring life to our hearts. There are many ways that God comforts us. We then can one day share this comfort with others who need to experience God's presence during hard times.

Lord, I bring all of my emotions before you and ask you meet me in my feeling of loss. Allow me to feel your presence, so that I know I am not alone. Help me to comfort those around me who need it, in the same way you have shown me comfort.

A Reminder to Remember

This is what the LORD Almighty said: "Administer true justice; show mercy and compassion to one another. Do not oppress the widow or the fatherless, the foreigner or the poor. Do not plot evil against each other."

ZECHARIAH 7:9-10 NIV

In times when people couldn't rely on writing a list or setting a reminder on their phone, they would sometimes tie strings around their index finger to remind them that something should be remembered. The string was a symbol to remember.

The Scripture is full of reminders that we should show mercy and compassion to those who are really in need. God had to continue to remind his people to take care of the widow, fatherless, foreigner, and poor. You might have a lot to get done today and you will have ways to remind yourself to do them. Will you find a symbol to remind you of the less fortunate? If you are feeling like you need a little help today, why don't you ask God to remind someone of your need.

Dear Lord, thank you for reminding me today that there are people in this world that are less fortunate than I am. Show me ways that I can show compassion to these people. I need your mercy and compassion so that I can be ready to love others, as you love me.

Convinced of Love

I am convinced that neither death, nor life, nor angels, nor rulers, nor
things present, nor things to come, nor powers, nor height, nor depth, nor
anything else in all creation, will be able to separate us from
the love of God in Christ Jesus our Lord.

ROMANS 8:38-39 NRSV

Love, in human terms, can become very conditional. We show love when
we feel good about someone, or when they have earned our respect
and trust. We find it harder to show love when we have been betrayed,
dismayed, or even disobeyed! Anger, hurt, and pride can easily separate us
from others.

Authentic love, from God, has been demonstrated to us through Jesus
Christ. We know that he laid down his life for all humanity and that his
sacrifice was not conditional on those who deserve it. For those of us
who have chosen to accept his grace, we can be *convinced* that nothing
will separate us from his love. Nothing. Your heavenly Father loves you,
completely and unconditionally.

*Thank you Jesus, for showing your love through your
sacrifice for me. I know that I am forgiven, and I know
that I am loved. Help me to walk in a way that is convinced t
hat nothing will keep me from your love.*

Increase of Love

This is my prayer: that your love may abound more and more in knowledge and depth of insight, so that you may be able to discern what is best and may be pure and blameless for the day of Christ.

PHILIPPIANS 1:9-10 NIV

We can hear over and over that God loves us, but sometimes it just takes time or a personal revelation to really understand the depth of his love. The Bible says that God *is* love and therefore the more we understand our God, the more we understand his love. As you gain insight into God's favor toward you and others, God gives you discernment and guidance to know what is best for your life.

Are you struggling with certain life decisions? Are you finding it hard to accept God's best for you? Allow yourself to soak in the depth of Christ's redeeming love. Then understand that he wants us to imitate this love. This is how we know what is best—when we make decisions out of love for Jesus and love for others.

Lord God, there is so much that I do not know or understand of you. But I know that you are love. Increase my knowledge of the depth of your love. Help me to discern what is best for my life by imitating the love you have shown me.

More than Enough

God is able to provide you with every blessing in abundance, so that by always having enough of everything, you may share abundantly in every good work.

2 CORINTHIANS 9:8 NRSV

Most of us don't feel like we have a lot to give, especially in the way of finances, resources, or time. Remember the story of the widow who only had enough flour and oil to make one last meal for herself and her son? When the prophet Elijah asked for her to make him bread out of this, she became worried. This would likely be our response as well.

What we often forget when God asks us to give of ourselves, is that he has already supplied the means. All God requires is our willingness to participate in his good work. We might think of abundance as exceeding wealth, but it is really saying that we have more than what is needed. If God asks of your time, then you can assume that he has given you more. If he asks of your money, he has given you more than enough. The widow became abundantly blessed by her willingness to give of what she had, and God saw that she was never in want again.

Lord, thank you for giving me more than enough of everything. I want to be willing to share what you have given me, and trust that you will make sure that I remain abundantly blessed. I give what I have to you.

Chosen

The LORD GOD gave me the ability to teach
so that I know what to say to make the weak strong.
Every morning he wakes me.
He teaches me to listen like a student.

ISAIAH 50:4 NCV

It's easy to wonder if we play a significant part in the kingdom of God. We question our own usefulness because we feel weak, inconsistent, and incapable of representing the perfect Savior of the world. But God gives us the ability to teach others. He fills our mouths with the words needed to bring life. In and of ourselves we may be weak and inadequate, but the Lord has more than compensated for our inabilities.

God has chosen you to be his messenger: the hands and feet and mouthpiece of his glory. He knows that you aren't perfect, but he is perfecting you every single moment through his grace and his redemptive love. Learn from him eagerly and serve him passionately. Your impact reaches further than you know.

Thank you, Jesus, for choosing me to impact the world for you.
Thank you for the gifts I have through you.
Help me to be faithful to teach others
what I've learned from your love.

Complete Confidence

I rejoice, because I have complete confidence in you.
2 CORINTHIANS 7:16 ESV

There are some things in our lives that we can put neatly into little boxes and organize into safely categorized compartments. We know how each of those things fits into our plans. But there are other things that no matter how hard we try to grab hold of, we can never fully regulate. Life, and all of its messy, unplanned circumstances can knock us right off our feet and disintegrate even the most perfectly laid plans. We can lose the control we spent our whole lives building in a single instant.

We can never place our confidence in our own ability to maintain control. Only when we place our full trust in God, abandoning our own preconceptions, can we have true joy in this life. Attempting to control the uncontrollable is as exhausting as it is impossible. We will never fully walk in freedom until we give up the need to make ourselves free.

God, I want the joy and the freedom that comes with putting my complete and utter confidence in your ability to guide and direct the outcome of my life. I need you to lead me. I cannot make my decisions in this life without you.

Establish Your Heart

You also be patient. Establish your hearts,
for the coming of the Lord is at hand.

JAMES 5:8 NKJV

We can decide on something in our minds and have the full intention to follow through, only to lose resolve when our heart is pulled elsewhere. The human heart is easily changed. It's driven by emotion and desire. Distractions of the world will readily try to shift our focus. That is why as children of God who are preparing for Christ's return, we must firmly plant our hearts in his truth—establishing ourselves on his Word in love.

If you keep your mind fixated on the promise of God and your heart established in the hope of eternity, then any other purpose will lose its appeal. The reality of the greatness that is ahead of you will so completely outweigh the attraction of what's distracting you. Establish yourself firmly in the Word of God, memorizing Scripture and meditating on truth, so that your divine purpose is always forefront in your heart.

Lord God, write your Word on my heart. Keep your truth continually in my mind. Establish me firmly in your presence so I will not be distracted by anything that tries to redirect my heart from you.

DAY 172

Nothing of My Own

He is so rich in kindness and grace that he purchased our freedom with the blood of his Son and forgave our sins.

EPHESIANS 1:7 NLT

When we let down our guard and pretenses, and we truly open our hearts and minds before God, we cannot help but feel exposed in his sight. Everything we've said, everything we've thought, everything we've done is known by him. But in that vulnerability, we must understand that no matter what we've done that day, that week, that year, we are simply seen in his eyes as beloved.

It is hard for us to humanly comprehend the truth that there is nothing we can do to make God love us any more or any less. This truth which, in theory, should remarkably free us, ultimately scares us. We know that we are completely out of control. The beauty is that grace will always be his work—and nothing of our own.

Heavenly Father, thank you for your grace.
Thank you that no matter what I've done, you will
only see your Son's redemption when you look at me.
Thank you for the grace I can't understand, and the
love I'm so deeply enveloped in.

Powerful Words

"Son of man, let all my words sink deep into your own heart first.
Listen to them carefully for yourself."

EZEKIEL 3:10 NLT

There is so much power in quieting our minds and listening to the voice
of God as he speaks directly to us. We must learn to recognize his voice
above any other sound. God has the power and the ability to speak to
any situation we are going through, under any circumstance.

Since the beginning of time, God has begun powerful works with a
powerful Word. When we listen for him to speak, we ready ourselves
for him to do those works in and through us.

*Lord, I want to be someone who does powerful works for your
kingdom. I know that I cannot do them without the words from your
mouth. Let me be a listener who both absorbs your Word
and is changed by it.*

Standing at the Last

LORD, you are my God;
I will exalt you and praise your name,
for in perfect faithfulness
you have done wonderful things.
things planned long ago.

ISAIAH 25:1 NIV

We serve a God who at the end, after everything has fallen and everything has changed, will still stand. In all of our confusion, suffering, and hopelessness, we have the enduring promise of serving the one who will always be greater.

It's easy to become discouraged in this life, but when we adjust our perspective to view everything against the backdrop of a victorious Savior, we can face absolutely anything with great confidence and peace.

Thank you, Lord, that in you, I can have the confidence of a victorious outcome—no matter how great the obstacles are that I am facing. Help me walk as one who is assured of my victory, trusting fully in my Savior who won it for me.

Unpunished

He has not punished us as our sins should be punished;
he has not repaid us for the evil we have done.

PSALM 103:10 NCV

We deserve death, punishment, and distance from God because of our sin.
But through the grace of salvation we have life, reward, and relationship
with God. While the devil condemns us because of our sin and causes us to
think that we have lost favor with God, the Holy Spirit convicts us of our sin
and leads us to repentance and greater favor.

There isn't any condemnation for us in Christ Jesus because he died to
remove our sin, our guilt, and our shame.

*Thank you Jesus that, because of your death on the cross, I can
stand blameless in the sight of Almighty God. I pray that I would be
sensitive to the Holy Spirit's gentle conviction, but would overcome
the devil's harsh condemnation because I am in Christ—a new
creation, free of guilt and shame.*

Do You Believe

"Everyone who lives and believes in me shall never die.
Do you believe this?"
JOHN 11:26 ESV

All throughout Scripture we are clearly promised eternal life through Christ. But there is something so poignant about the question in this verse: "Do you believe this?" Do you really, truly believe that you will live forever in heaven with Christ?

We are accustomed to promises being made and broken daily. Human fallacy has left us skeptical and anxious. But the beautiful truth is that we serve a God who will never back out of his covenant with us. Our hope of eternal life is sealed for us when we place our trust in Christ.

Thank you, heavenly Father, for eternal life that is given to me through your Son. I do believe in you and in what you have promised me. Calm my fears and strengthen my faith. Enable me to live my life in you, relying on your strength and resting in your great love.

Accomplishment

LORD, you will grant us peace;
all we have accomplished is really from you.
ISAIAH 26:12 NLT

As we each look back on our lives, we remember what we've accomplished with some sense of pride. We have all climbed our mountains, but here we are—still standing to tell the tale.

As we reflect with peace in our hearts on things past, we must remember that we could have done none of it without God. He is the one who carries our burdens, comforts our hearts, strengthens our resolve, and orders our steps.

Thank you, Lord, that you have been there for me every step of the way. I would have nothing if it weren't for you. Thank you for the peace that you give me and for the works that you've done in me. I look forward to what you have yet to accomplish in my life.

DAY 178

Unseen

We do not look at what we can see right now, the troubles all around us, but we look forward to the joys in heaven which we have not yet seen. The troubles will soon be over, but the joys to come will last forever.

2 CORINTHIANS 4:18 TLB

It's not easy to fix our eyes on something we can't see. By abandoning our earthly perspective in exchange for a heavenly one, we are radically changed. If we are focused only on what is here on earth, we will quickly find ourselves overwhelmed by fear and uncertainty.

If we fix our eyes on the promise of heaven, then we cannot help but be filled with peace, joy, and hope. We must remember that while we are here on earth for only a little while, it is the joy of heaven that will be our eternal, blessed reality.

Lord, help me to fix my eyes on you and on eternity rather than on the momentary troubles around me. Give me your perspective.

Life of Laughter

He will once again fill your mouth with laughter
and your lips with shouts of joy.

JOB 8:21 NLT

When was the last time you shouted with joy? It seems as the years go by, we find ourselves with more responsibility, more tasks, more heartache, and often more conflict. Our body gets tired, our minds grow weary, and our emotions are spent. It is important in times of heaviness that we find reasons to smile and laugh.

God created laughter, and he is the source of true joy. If you are feeling like there is not enough joy in your life, take time to reflect on God's love for you. Understand that he is a merciful God. Know that he delights in you. Dwell on the beauty of his creation. Thank him for the good relationships that he has brought into your life. Find him in a song, or a dance, or the smile of a child. When you seek God, you will find what you need. Let him once again fill your mouth with laugher.

Dear God, I want to feel joy again in my life. I want to be a person that reflects the deep joy that is experienced by knowing you. Remind me of things today that are good reasons to smile. Fill my mouth with laughter, and my lips with shouts of joy.

Father of Light

Whatever is good and perfect comes to us from God,
the Creator of all light, and he shines forever without change or shadow.

JAMES 1:17 TLB

In the beginning, the earth was void and darkness was on the face of the deep. God transformed this darkness with a command: "Let there be light." God saw the light and declared it good. Light is a magnificent part of God's creation. It reflects some of God's nature in that it dispels darkness; nothing hides in the light.

Our heavenly Father is perfect and therefore he is able to give you good and perfect things. You may already feel blessed by his goodness or you may wonder if you have received anything perfect from him. If you doubt his goodness (which is okay at times), remember that he has given you perfect love and grace in the form of Jesus Christ. Nothing can change his love; nothing can cast a shadow on his mercy. Allow this truth to permeate your heart.

Heavenly Father, thank you that you created light,
and that you are a light in my world. Thank you for
showing me that you are a good and merciful God.
Help me to accept that your goodness toward
me will never change.

Lift Up Your Leaders

Obey those who rule over you, and be submissive, for they watch out for
your souls, as those who must give account. Let them do so with joy and
not with grief, for that would be unprofitable for you.

HEBREWS 13:17 NKJV

In a society where we can pick and choose according to personal
preference, our church leaders do not stand much of a chance when
submitted to critique. How often do we walk away from a sermon,
teaching, or conversation with a leader and pick out what we didn't like
about it?

It is true that church leaders can lie, cheat, and gossip as much as anyone
else. Many great leaders have fallen prey to great sin and cannot be trusted
anymore. However, there are also many wonderful men and women of God
who are living out their calling to "feed his sheep" and "make disciples of
all people." These are the leaders that need our prayer and encouragement.
God has placed these people over you to watch out for your soul. Are you
praying for your leaders, or just complaining about them? Be respectful to
those God has put over you; learn to be helpful, not a hindrance!

*Dear Lord, I'm sorry when I have complained too much about my
church leaders, or those in authority over me.
I pray for them now, Lord, that you would strengthen them. Help
them to maintain integrity and give them grace as they lead.*

Remedy for the Weary

He gives strength to the weary
and increases the power of the weak.

ISAIAH 40:29 NIV

When you are suffering from any form of bodily sickness, your body puts most of its effort into fighting the illness. As a result, you feel tired and weak, sometimes to the point of not being able to get out of bed. This analogy is a good way to understand how our heart and emotions can feel weary and weak when we are dealing with the pressures and difficulties of life.

What is the remedy for your weariness and weakness? Jesus. He is the one who can mend a broken relationship. Provide for your needs. Give you patience when you are angry, and peace when you are anxious. God is your friend when you are lonely, and your Father when you need protection. Trust him for all of these things and your soul will find strength and vitality to live to the fullest.

Jesus, on those days when I am tired and weak,
remind me that you are everything I need.
Thank you that you care about the weary and the
weak, and that your love and power can lift me up
in the times I need it most. Grant me your strength today.

Prayerful Union

They all met together and were constantly united in prayer, along with
Mary the mother of Jesus, several other women, and the brothers of Jesus.

ACTS 1:14 NLT

Imagine what it would have been like to be those women who gathered
with the apostles at the very beginning of the early church. It would have
been exciting to experience the presence and power of the Holy Spirit.
Excitement would also have been mixed with fears, doubts, and quite
possibly the ridicule of outsiders. Nevertheless, all the followers of Jesus
were united and prayed together often. Here, there was no distinction
between people groups or gender. All could play a part in establishing
God's kingdom on earth.

It is important to remember that God desires unity in the church in the same
way that the early apostles did. If you are part of a church or community of
believers, then your presence and affirmation is needed to encourage the
church. Don't let the enemy tell you that you are insignificant, or that you
don't need to attend that prayer meeting. Actively engage with other Christ
followers so that you can be encouraged as well.

*Thank you, Lord, for the believers you have placed around me. Help
me to do my best to create unity with them and to encourage their
faith. Give us a desire to pray together so we can all be stirred
to do your work in this world.*

Purposeful Plans

Listen to advice and accept discipline,
and at the end you will be counted among the wise.
Many are the plans in a person's heart,
but it is the LORD's purpose that prevails.

PROVERBS 19:20-21 NIV

"Lord, nothing has been going to plan lately." It's a prayer that you may
have prayed recently, or can certainly empathize with. Some of us like to
plan everything right down to the finest detail. If you aren't one of these
people, you still have plans in your heart about your goals and desires in life.

The problem is not with the planning; the problem is when you don't
include God in the plans. God is the author of life; therefore, he is the one
that writes your story. He has a purpose for your life. Your job is to walk
alongside him so you fulfill that purpose. It can be tough to know what he
wants you do to, even on a day-to-day basis, but a good way to find out is to
listen to wise advice and accept God's correction when you get it wrong. Be
wise and his plans for your life will succeed!

*Dear Lord, I have been frustrated lately when things haven't gone
the way I would have liked them to. I pray you would help me
to include you more in my plans, so I can live wisely.*

Lasting Love

Give thanks to the LORD, for he is good;
his love endures forever.

1 CHRONICLES 16:34 NIV

Romantic relationships come and go; people can be in love one day and out of it the next! When love is approached selfishly, relationships are abandoned when there is no longer a benefit. This can even happen in friendships. If you have been through this kind of heartache, you may be a bit cynical about love.

If selfish love easily ends, then it must be unselfish love that endures. We know from the Scriptures that Jesus was the ultimate example of selflessness. Jesus sacrificed his life on the cross because of his great love for us. This is a love that gives preference to others and always seeks their best. Do you need to be reminded that God's love for you is enduring? He is good and therefore his love for you is pure and unfailing.

*Lord, I thank you that you love me with an everlasting love.
Let me be reminded today of your goodness and faithfulness to me.
At times I have felt disappointed by love, but I thank you that my
hope can be restored because of your great love.*

Give Me Liberty

Now you are free from the power of sin and have become slaves of God.
Now you do those things that lead to holiness and result in eternal life.

ROMANS 6:22 NLT

Freedom is a place without obligations. Freedom is to live exempt from
debts, constraints, and bonds. Our obligation for the sin we've committed
is to satisfy justice. Our souls cannot be free without a release
from our debt of sin, and the currency demanded
for a soul is death.

When our debt was paid by the death of Jesus, the truest form of freedom
was declared over our soul. Our chains were broken, and our liberty was
granted. When Jesus returned to heaven, he left his spirit with us because
where his spirit is, there is freedom.

*Father, thank you for the freedom that is waiting for me as
I walk out of sin. Jesus, you have paid the price for my sin once
and for all, and I am eternally grateful for your sacrifice.*

One of Us

Rather, he made himself nothing
by taking the very nature of a servant,
being made in human likeness.
PHILIPPIANS 2:7 NIV

When we face hardships in life we can often feel like nobody really relates to what we are going through. Sometimes people cannot see beyond their own situation to know how to help. Perhaps you have been in a situation where you didn't really know how to help a friend who was going through a really tough time.

We need to be reminded that Jesus knew what it was like to be human. He didn't come as a god among men; he came in human form. This means he experienced physical things like hunger and tiredness, as well as emotions like sadness and excitement. If anyone knows about suffering, it is Jesus. If you are feeling like you need empathy for your situation, look to him; he understands.

Jesus, thank you for experiencing humanity on earth,
so you are able to completely understand my
difficulties. You already know my circumstances,
so I simply ask that I will sense your presence
in my life, knowing that you care deeply for me.

Jailhouse Rock

About midnight Paul and Silas were praying and singing hymns to God,
and the prisoners were listening to them.

ACTS 16:25 NRSV

Being thrown into prison for your faith is one of the hardest forms of
persecution believers can face. It is worth noticing that despite the walls
around them, Paul and Silas continued to praise God with praying and
singing. It must have been loud enough for the other prisoners to hear
them. Paul and Silas were able to be a witness in the most severe of
circumstances.

We are a light to the world and God uses us in many different ways. Perhaps
you have had it tough lately, or maybe things are going very well. Either
way, people are listening. Who are the prisoners around you that need
to be set free by the love of Christ? Who needs to hear your prayers and
singing? Can you trust that God is good wherever you are in life right now?
He will give you strength to praise him at all times.

*Father God, thank you that you are with me in all circumstances. Help
me to remember that what I say and do can encourage others around
me. Give me boldness to praise you as a witness to others.*

Released and Restored

He was pierced for our transgressions,
he was crushed for our iniquities;
the punishment that brought us peace was on him,
and by his wounds we are healed.

ISAIAH 53:5 NIV

When a judge puts down the hammer to seal a guilty verdict, the person is condemned to whatever sentence is given. Forms of punishment have been different over time and space, but they all share the same purpose— to cause one to suffer as a consequence for wrongdoing. We were all that guilty person under the hammer once. We were cursed by the sin of humanity.

What a powerful transformation it was when Jesus came to remove the curse. He suffered to release us from guilt. His punishment brought us peace. He wore the shame so we could be healed. While it is sobering to realize what Jesus has done for us, we can also rejoice in our freedom. Jesus is not still on the cross! We are not still under the curse! If you are feeling the weight of your brokenness today, let your heart be encouraged that Jesus came to give you life. Live in the fullness of his love!

*Lord Jesus, thank you that you have released me
from the curse of sin so that I can live in forgiveness
and healing. I bring all of my hurt and shame to
you today and pray that you would restore me
to health and wholeness.*

Measured Days

LORD, let me know my end,
and what is the measure of my days;
let me know how fleeting my life is.

PSALM 39:4 NRSV

Life throws all kinds of things at us. Stress, pressure, decisions, and busy schedules. When we are living, rushed in the midst of our own lives, we forget the age-old reality that life passes very quickly. If we stop—as the Psalmist did—in full awareness of a fleeting life, we begin to recognize that what was once pressing is really trivial, and what was once urgent is actually insignificant.

By numbering our days and being mindful of our own fleeting existence on earth, we can spend our energies not on the pressures of earth, but rather on the purposes of heaven, which will last forever.

Teach me, Lord, to number my days. Give me eternal vision so that I can live my life for the things that truly matter and not spend so much of my time pursuing what won't last.

Not Shaken

Cast your burden upon the LORD and He will sustain you;
He will never allow the righteous to be shaken.

PSALM 55:22 NASB

We all have different ways of dealing with worry. Some internalize it, others call a friend, and still others find a way to take their minds off it. When we bring our worry to God and lay our anxious hearts bare before him, he will encourage us, lift us up, and sustain us. He will not allow us to be shaken or weakened by worry because he holds us through every situation.

The God who knows beginning from end is not flustered by our anxiety, and does not allow us to be overcome by uncertainty.

Thank you, God, that you welcome me to come to you when I am burdened. You don't want me to carry my anxiety alone. My future is secure in your hands, and all I have to do is rest in you.

Never Disappointed

This hope will never disappoint us, because God has poured out
his love to fill our hearts. He gave us his love through the Holy Spirit,
whom God has given to us.

ROMANS 5:5 NCV

None of us are strangers to being disappointed. In life, we have learned
to prepare ourselves for both the best and the worst possible outcomes.
But when it comes to our salvation, there is no need to be braced for
disappointment because the hope we have in Christ is guaranteed.

The presence of the Holy Spirit in our hearts reminds us constantly of this
beautiful, certain promise we have in Christ.

Thank you, God, that the hope I have in you will not lead me to
disappointment. No matter how many times I am let down in this
world, I know that your love will never fail me.

Guided

I will lead the blind
by a road they do not know,
by paths they have not known
I will guide them.
I will turn the darkness before them into light,
the rough places into level ground.
These are the things I will do,
and I will not forsake them.

ISAIAH 42:16 NRSV

When you feel that you have lost your way, and your feet can't feel the path beneath you, God promises that he will lead you forward. Even if you can't see what lies ahead, and though the road feels rocky and unsure, God will guide you. The path that seemed impassable will become smooth and the way that seemed impossible will become straightforward.

God promises that he will do this for you and more—because he loves you and his is a love that never fails or forsakes.

***Thank you for your promise to guide me
no matter how impossible the way seems.***

God of Safety

Those who go to God Most High for safety
will be protected by the Almighty.
I will say to the LORD,
"You are my place of safety and protection.
You are my God and I trust you."

PSALM 91:1-2 NCV

We all applaud the heroism of the young boy David when he took on the giant, Goliath. Or the boldness of Moses when he confronted Pharaoh about freeing the Israelites. But do we recognize that the same safety given to them has been given to us? They were regular people like us, who understood the power of the God they served.

Whatever you are facing right now, God is more than able to rescue you and keep you safe in the midst of it.

God, I want to have the kind of radical trust that these Biblical heroes had. Give me the boldness that I need to be a believer who walks in your power.

Cleansed

Have mercy upon me, O God,
According to Your lovingkindness;
According to the multitude of Your tender mercies,
Blot out my transgressions.
Wash me thoroughly from my iniquity,
And cleanse me from my sin.

PSALM 51:1-2 NKJV

We should all long to be purified of our sin because it is in the cleansing from our iniquity that we are brought nearer to God. Our sin may be precious to us, but when we compare it to the treasure of closeness with the Father, it instantly loses its worth.

God doesn't harden his heart to a repentant believer. When we cry out to him in genuine remorse, he lavishes us with his mercy and love, washing us of our sin and restoring us to right relationship with him.

Have mercy on me, God. Remove my sin from me and cleanse me so that I can be closer to you.

Without Fear of the Future

She is clothed with strength and dignity,
and she laughs without fear of the future.

PROVERBS 31:25 NLT

It's natural to fear the unknown. It can be frightening not to know what's coming or how to prepare for it. But you don't have to fear the future when you know whom you trust. You can live without anxiety about what is to come because you know that your life is in the hands of the one who controls it all.

When you are in Christ, you can smile at the mystery of the future with the peaceful and carefree heart of one who knows it is secure.

God, give me the strength to smile at the days to come. Don't let me waste my moments in fear of things that fear can never change. Grant me the peace that comes with trusting you.

A Greater Wonder

When I look at your heavens, the work of your fingers,
the moon and the stars, which you have set in place,
what is man that you are mindful of him,
and the son of man that you care for him?

PSALM 8:3-4 ESV

The greatness of our God is displayed majestically throughout his creation. When we look into the night sky at all the twinkling stars and the far off planets, we realize almost instantly how small we are in his universe. But a greater wonder than the grandeur of God's capacity is his value for mankind.

The God of all this—the universe and everything in it—is the same God who gave his life to know us. The God who spoke the world into being is the same God who speaks quietly to our hearts. His love for us is as unsearchable as the heavens.

Father, I don't understand why you love me
the way you do when you are as great as you are.
But I am so thankful you do.

Trustworthy

For the word of the LORD holds true,
and we can trust everything he does.
PSALM 33:4 NLT

All of us have experienced our fair share of hurt. We've been jaded by failed dreams, broken relationships, and empty promises. No matter how hurt or worn down we may feel, we can always trust God with our hearts. He will never lie to us, manipulate us, or let us down. He will never go back on his word to us, abandon us, or stop loving us.

The Lord is always true to his Word. Who he has been throughout the ages is who he remains today. The God we read about in Scripture—who never forgot his covenants and loved irrevocably—is the same God who holds our hearts today.

Thank you, Lord, that in a world where trust is broken daily, I can always trust you perfectly. Please heal my heart from the hurt I've experienced so that I can love you more deeply.

Fascination

Those who love your teachings will find true peace,
and nothing will defeat them.
PSALM 119:165 NCV

The natural result of love is fascination: to be drawn to something so irresistibly that nothing can keep you from it. When we fascinate ourselves with the Word of God, we become an indestructible force in the spiritual realm.

We cannot be easily subjected to the lies of the enemy when our hearts have been saturated in the truth. By loving the teachings of God, his wisdom becomes our confidence and his presence our reward.

God, give me a love for your teachings. When my flesh rises up against your truth, help me to overcome it by your Spirit. Let me be fascinated by you. Give me a love for you and your Word that is unmatched by any other love in my life.

Joyfully I Wait

I wait for the LORD, my whole being waits,
and in his word I put my hope.

PSALM 130:5 NIV

We so often think of waiting as hard, even unpleasant. But sometimes, waiting is wonderful: waiting to deliver great news, waiting for the birth of a child, the anticipation of giving a special gift.

When the thing we wait for is a good thing, waiting itself is a gift. This is how it is to wait for the Lord. With all our hope in him, the outcome is certain. The outcome is eternity. Let every part of us wait on him in joyful anticipation.

Lord, I love waiting for you! Because I know you bring only goodness, I can wait for you forever. Your Word is my hope, and it promises light and life forever with you. Gratefully, joyfully, I wait and I hope.

Good and Perfect

Whatever is good and perfect is a gift coming down to us from God our
Father, who created all the lights in the heavens. He never changes
or casts a shifting shadow.

JAMES 1:17 NLT

Take the next few minutes to pause and consider all the good, all the
beauty in your life. You may be in a season that makes this easy, or perhaps
now is a time that doesn't feel particularly "good and perfect."

Peonies in June, the wink of a quarter moon, loving and being loved, these
are gifts from God. Your Father is a good father, a giver of good gifts. This
doesn't change, even when your circumstances do.

*Lord, every day you send gifts, reminding me you are good and I am
yours. Help me see your gifts even through tears. You are constant;
you are perfect. Thank you for loving me.*

Tears Turn to Joy

Those who sow in tears
shall reap with shouts of joy!
PSALM 126:5 ESV

In times of sadness, whether from a fresh heartbreak or the memory of a distant one, it can seem like the pain will never end. No words of comfort, no matter how true or well-intentioned, can take away the ache.

These are the times we need only to crawl into our Abba's lap and allow his love and promises to envelop us in comfort. He won't say when, but he does assure us: we will shout again for joy.

Father, there are days it is just too much. This world brings so much difficulty, challenge, and sadness; I just want to lie in your arms. How wonderful to know that I can! You hold me tightly and whisper your promises in my ear: "You will laugh again. You might cry today, but one day, you will shout for joy."

Unconditional Acceptance

Accept one another, then, just as Christ accepted you,
in order to bring praise to God.

ROMANS 15:7 NIV

If she gossiped less. If he shared his feelings more.
It's easy, isn't it, to list the ways other people could change for the better?
We know we are called to live in harmony with one another, but our
"others" can really make it difficult.

But we need to accept one another… as Christ accepted us. Jesus takes us
as we are: broken, imperfect, sinful. If this is how the Savior welcomes us,
who are we to put conditions on our acceptance of anyone else?

*Lord, thank you for accepting me just as I am. You see past my many
flaws and you love me for me. Help me to see others as you see them
and to glorify you through unconditional acceptance.*

A Heart That Cares

God is working in you, giving you the desire
and the power to do what pleases him.

PHILIPPIANS 2:13 NLT

What was your last random act of kindness? Whether you bought a
homeless man a burger, donated to dig a new well in Africa, or simply
smiled at a stranger in the produce aisle, these impulses are evidence
of the Spirit at work in your life.

The more we tune into God, the more he will work in us. As we focus our
thoughts on his perfect love and look to him for inspiration, he provides us
with opportunities—big and small—to express his love to others.

*God, today I thank you for giving me a heart that cares. Help me to see
and to seize the opportunities you place before me to share your love
and goodness, today and every day.*

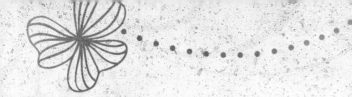

He Never Sleeps

He will not let you stumble;
the one who watches over you will not slumber.

PSALM 121:3 NLT

How long can you go without sleep? Most of us have gone all night at least once, but we also collapsed, exhausted, as soon as we were able. No matter how important the task, how critical the vigil, we all have to take a break eventually.

All except God. The one who watches over you, the one who makes sure you won't stumble as you climb today's mountain, never stops watching. Always and forever, night and day, he's got you.

Father, I marvel today at the realization that you never take your eyes off me. You have my eternity in your heart, and you won't let me fall. Whatever my mistakes, you are awake and ready to guide me back to the right path. Thank you, Lord, for your constant presence.

No Darkness

This is the message we have heard from him and declare to you: God is light; in him there is no darkness at all.

1 JOHN 1:5 NIV

In total darkness, we instinctively seek light. We turn on our phones, fumble for a light switch, light a candle. With a single light source, the darkness can be overcome. We can find our way.

This same principle applies to our hearts. God is pure light, and with him, we can overcome any darkness we face. No temptation, no addiction, no sin is too powerful for God to conquer.

Father, I know that whenever and wherever I face darkness,
I need only seek your face. You are all good, all pure, all light.
I surrender my struggle with the darkness to you, and ask you
to help me overcome it. I want to live in your pure light.

He Chose You

The LORD is all I need.
He takes care of me.
My share in life has been pleasant;
my part has been beautiful.

PSALM 16:5-6 NCV

If you are a follower of Christ, God chose precisely when and how to invite you to join his family. You received the most prestigious, coveted invitation in history. He chose you.

Maybe you simply yearned for more meaning in your life and he led you into a Christian community. Perhaps you needed a radical life change, to shed an addiction or other destructive pattern, and you felt him lift you out of the darkness. Regardless of how it happened, he called you by name, and now you are his.

Lord, I'll never get over it: you chose me.
You pulled me out of darkness, into light and love and hope.
I am yours, today and forever. Thank you!

You Are Chosen

God decided in advance to adopt us into his own family
by bringing us to himself through Jesus Christ. This is what
he wanted to do, and it gave him great pleasure.

EPHESIANS 1:5 NLT

Adopted children never have to wonder if they were wanted. They grow up with the certainty that their parents chose them. What a blessing.

As a child of God, you are granted that same wonderful knowledge. You are his adopted one, chosen specially to bring him pleasure. Not to accomplish any great feat, or to fulfill any grand purpose, but just because he wanted you.

Father, I can't believe you chose me. With all my faults and all the times I go my own way, I'm amazed you call me your beloved child. Knowing I bring pleasure to you just by being me is one of the great joys of my life.

He Will Shelter You

He will cover you with his feathers.
He will shelter you with his wings.
His faithful promises are your armor and protection.

PSALM 91:4 NLT

Like an eagle, God shelters us beneath his wings from storms and attacks.
The image is powerful, yet also tender. How wonderful it is to be tucked in,
right up against him, absorbing his warmth!

Do you rest in this promise of protection, or do you struggle, always poking
your head out to see what dangers await? Maybe you've even tried to
leave the nest altogether and take care of yourself. If so, return to his side.
Accept his protection.

*Lord, you are my shelter. Thank you for providing me a safe, warm
place to wait out life's storms. Forgive me for the times I resist you,
believing I can do it alone. Your wings are my armor,
and they are mighty to save.*

Peace and Quiet

The work of righteousness will be peace,
And the effect of righteousness,
quietness and assurance forever.

ISAIAH 32:17 NKJV

Peace and quiet. Just saying those words together can bring comfort.
It can also bring despair, if they seem out of reach. How, oh how can we
claim them?

Through righteousness comes peace, quietness, and assurance. Forever.
It's a big word, righteousness, and one you may have shied away from.
If so, lean in. Righteousness is not an unattainable ideal of perfection or
superiority. It's about putting God first, and living in a way that honors him.
In exchange for your honor, he offers the peace and quiet you long for.

Lord, I want to live a righteous life. Not just for the peace you offer in
return, or the quiet assurance of your love for me, but because you
are God, wholly deserving of my honor and devotion.

Why

As you do not know the path of the wind,
or how the body is formed in a mother's womb,
so you cannot understand the work of God,
the Maker of all things.

ECCLESIASTES 11:5 NIV

"Why?" Call to mind a toddler who has just grasped the meaning and power of this wonderful little word. Over and over, to everything they hear, they respond, "Why?"

As we grow we learn to stop asking why so often, but inside our minds, we maintain a powerful desire to know. It is human nature. However, when it comes to the mind of God, we cannot satisfy this desire. His mind—his ways—cannot be known. Accepting and even embracing this truth is a sign of spiritual growth.

Father, I long to know you! Even regarding that which
I cannot know, my soul cries out, "But why?"
Please help me enjoy the wondering, Lord.
Help me rest in your sovereignty.

Coffee with God

I rise before dawn and cry for help;
I wait for Your words.
PSALM 119:147 NASB

How is morning for you? Do you rise before you need to, eager to start your day, or is the snooze button your best friend? If you are in the former group, do you begin your day with God?

Numerous times in Scripture, we are encouraged to be morning people. For some, this advice is not even necessary; for others, it seems impossibly out of reach. "I'm just not wired that way," we say. Perhaps, if this is us, a rewiring is in order. If you knew you had a coffee date with the Father, would you even need an alarm?

Lord, I don't want to miss a minute with you. Beginning my day in your Word, soaking up your wisdom, is a joy and a privilege. Whether for the first or the thousand and first time, I desire to spend the first minutes of every day alone with you.

Real Love

Since ancient times no one has heard,
no ear has perceived,
no eye has seen any God besides you,
who acts on behalf of those who wait for him.

ISAIAH 64:4 NIV

Authenticity. It matters, doesn't it? We wonder if the gem, the handbag, the promise, is real. We've all heard the expression, "If it's too good to be true, it's probably not," so we scrutinize the people and possessions in our lives, looking for authenticity.

What great comfort we can take in our God: the one, true God! All his promises are true; all his gifts are good. His love is authentic, and it is ours to claim.

Lord, you are God. The one, the only, the Almighty God. Who am I that you should act on my behalf, that you should speak into my life? And yet you do. May my love for you be authentic, may my words of praise be true.

Planner

Now devote your heart and soul to seeking
the LORD your God.
1 CHRONICLES 22:19 NIV

The month of August is one that creates a sense of eager anticipation. Summer is wrapping up, and with September usually comes new beginnings. There is excitement in the air as the school buses start up their engines, sports seasons get underway, and Labor Day plans come and go. August can be a great time to get into a routine.

August can mean that your mornings start just a half hour early to spend time in the presence of God. Or you find time in the afternoon to go for a quick walk to pray. Or you start a prayer chain with women you know to pray for one another as the months roll by. When you make dedicated time with the Lord, conversing with him becomes a part of your every day—a necessity to find your day complete. And oh, how it delights him when we spend time in his presence!

Lord, help me to be more intentional about meeting with you. I know you are always ready to spend time with me, and I want to make it a priority to be with you. Thank you for your patience with me and your gentle reminders that you are waiting.

Tell Your Story

Let the redeemed of the LORD tell their story—
those he redeemed from the hand of the foe.

PSALM 107:2 NIV

What's your story? Whether it's so complex you barely know where to begin, or you think it's too insignificant to tell, be assured that it matters.

From the beginning, God had you in mind. He planned you out to the tiniest detail. He has loved you forever. The way in which you discovered this beautiful truth, or the way it is currently unfolding, is of great significance. Begin telling it to yourself, and be ready to share it when the time comes.

Lord, when I consider your story, mine seems so small. That you chose me to be a part of it is too wonderful to comprehend. Thank you for my story, Father. May I learn to see it as you do: significant, beautiful, and worthy.

Opened, Lifted, and Loved

The LORD opens the eyes of the blind;
The LORD raises up those who are bowed down;
The LORD loves the righteous.

PSALM 146:8 NASB

Our God loves to restore life to his creation. When Jesus came to earth, he healed many physical needs. Greater than physical healing, Jesus came to restore our spiritual brokenness. He opened eyes to the truth, ministered to the poor in spirit, and restored believers to righteousness.

How blessed you are. He has opened your eyes, he will always lift you up in times of trouble, and he loves you because you have chosen the path of righteousness. Let the God of encouragement and restoration be your strength today.

God, you have opened my eyes to the truth; you have forgiven my sin, and you love me. Some days I have fallen harder than others, and today I need you to once again bring restoration to my body and soul. Thank you for picking me up and encouraging me on the path of righteousness.

His Riches

This same God who takes care of me will supply
all your needs from his glorious riches,
which have been given to us in Christ Jesus.

PHILIPPIANS 4:19 NLT

The Lord's riches are found in his goodness, his grace, and his sovereignty as king over all. God is always able to provide for all of our needs. Sometimes we may feel as though we are not worthy to receive from the Lord. Sometimes we find it hard to trust and we worry about our needs.

The good news of Jesus Christ is that he has given us access to the throne of God. You are a child of the King and he offers his riches to you. All you need to do is love him, ask him, and trust in his goodness. His promise is to take care of you.

Almighty God, you are sovereign and good. Thank you that you want to take care of me. There are things that I feel I need right now and I submit them to you. I pray you would take the burden from me as I continue to trust you each and every day.

Satisfied

Because your love is better than life,
my lips will glorify you.
I will praise you as long as I live,
and in your name I will lift up my hands.
I will be fully satisfied as with the richest of foods;
with singing lips my mouth will praise you.

PSALM 63:3-5 NIV

There are times in our lives when we really need answers or a breakthrough, and sometimes we just want to be blessed. Our loving Father says to simply ask.

God wants to give us good gifts. You might not want to ask for things because you feel they are too much, or too specific. But God is able to handle our requests—he won't give us things that will bring us harm or that we will use for our selfish gain. He knows what is best for us. His love is better than life itself, and he knows exactly how to satisfy us.

Lord, there are many things that I need and many things I want. I ask you for them now because I know that you are a loving Father who wants to answer me today.

Whole Restoration

My whole being, praise the LORD
and do not forget all his kindnesses.
He forgives all my sins
and heals all my diseases.

PSALM 103:2-3 NCV

Our God is a God of restoration. He shows us his kindness, through his love, in that he cares for our entire being. Not only does God want to restore a right relationship with you, he also wants to restore your body to health.

When we are spiritually or physically weak, we can sometimes forget the promises of God. In these times, think on his character; remember that he is a loving Father who wants the best for you. Praise him with all of your heart, soul, and mind, and watch him bring restoration to the areas of your life that need it the most.

Heavenly Father, I praise you with my whole being. I remember your kindness toward me, and I ask you to show me your mercy. Forgive my sins and renew my heart. Heal my body and restore my health.

Any Prayer Counts

Pray in the Spirit on all occasions with all kinds
of prayers and requests.
EPHESIANS 6:18 NIV

Often we are too analytical with our prayers. We think we ought to make
them sound fancy or humble. We can treat prayer like money: we don't
want to spend it on the wrong things. We might not be able to trust our
intentions when we pray, but God sees our heart.

The Lord wants you to talk with him in all occasions and with all kinds of
prayers. Sometimes our prayer is a quick cry for help, and sometimes it is an
hour-long worship session! No matter what kind of prayer, Jesus will always
be present to hear you.

*Jesus, I don't always know how to pray, how short or how informal
I can be, or what things are acceptable to pray for. I thank you for
reminding me that it doesn't actually matter. What matters is that I
open my heart to you at all times and acknowledge that I need you in
any and every area of my life.*

Opportunity for Joy

When troubles of any kind come your way, consider it
an opportunity for great joy. For you know that when your faith
is tested, your endurance has a chance to grow.

JAMES 1:2-3 NLT

It's not easy to approach troubles with joy, unless we can understand how these things work out for good. One of the best things that comes from trouble is that we are tested. And while testing seems like something to get anxious about, when we pass, we have more confidence than we had before.

Endurance is a quality that is crucial to staying true to our faith in the hard times. Rather than giving up when troubles come, hold onto your faith in Jesus and ask the Holy Spirit to help you in times of trouble.

Lord, there have been times lately where I feel that my faith is really being tested. Help me to consider my misfortunes as an opportunity to lean on you and develop my endurance. Give me joy in the middle of my trouble, knowing that better things are coming.

Quenched

The desert and the parched land will be glad;
the wilderness will rejoice and blossom.

ISAIAH 35:1 NIV

There are times in life when we feel like we are always striving and never getting anywhere; where we thirst for something more but still feel dry. God has promised that there will be a day when we, the redeemed, will no longer thirst for fulfillment; when everything we desire will be satisfied.

Before that day, however, God is still willing and able to grant you an oasis in the desert and give you signs of life in whatever kind of "wilderness" you may be experiencing. Just like the promise Jesus made to the woman at the well, the water that he gives is everlasting and becomes in us a spring of water welling up to eternal life.

God, thank you for the water that you give to satisfy my soul. I want to draw from your everlasting well so that I can endure the desert moments and experience growth in the times of wilderness.

Light of the Dawn

Even in darkness light dawns for the upright,
for those who are gracious and compassionate
and righteous.

PSALM 112:4 NIV

The middle of the night can be an anxious time to be awake, often bringing irrational fears of danger, disturbing thoughts, or a disquieted spirit. In contrast, the first rays of light in the morning can bring peace, hope, and joy.

Life does not always seem full of hope and joy, especially when you have experienced hurt, anxiety, or depression. God's truth, however, is that even in your moments of darkness his light will dawn for you. Grace, compassion, and righteousness belong to you as you allow Jesus to shine his life into your heart.

*Jesus, sometimes I despair over the darkness in this world.
In these times, I choose to trust in the light that you bring into
my life and into the world. Let me experience the hope
and joy that comes with the dawn.*

Thunder Theology

"God's voice thunders in marvelous ways;
he does great things beyond our understanding."

JOB 37:5 NIV

Thunder is powerful, mysterious, and commanding. It's little wonder that God's voice is described in this way. With his voice, he created the heavens and the earth. His voice can command all things into submission to his will.

Throughout history God has done great things, and he is able to do great things today. What are the great things that you have been asking for in your life? Do you believe that he can do them? Just like the thunder, we may not fully comprehend how God works, but we know that he is present and powerful. Trust him to do great things.

Almighty God, you created the heavens and the earth. You are powerful and worthy of my praise. Thank you for doing great things in my life and in the world around me. Teach me to worship you as the awesome God that you are.

Fiery Furnace

"If we are thrown into the blazing furnace, the God whom we serve
is able to save us. He will rescue us from your power, Your Majesty."

DANIEL 3:17 NLT

What confidence Shadrach, Meshach, and Abednego had in God's power to
rescue them from the blazing furnace! Not only did they refuse to worship
the king's idol, they willingly went through the fire to prove the power of
their God.

You are unlikely to have to go through literal flames for God, but he
will honor your decision to stand up for your faith in him. You may feel
pressured by the majority to live a certain way, to accept other religions,
and to compromise your standards. Be encouraged that our God is the God
who miraculously saved these faithful men from the fire, and he is the only
one worthy of praise.

*Dear God, give me faith as strong as these three men. Help me to
stand against the idols of this world and to hold fast to my belief in
you. I want to serve you for the rest of my days, and I ask for your
protection along the way.*

My Redeemer Lives

"I know that my Redeemer lives,
and at the last he will stand upon the earth."

JOB 19:25 ESV

If you are familiar with the story of Job, you will know that God allowed him to suffer greatly; he lost his family, his health, and his wealth. We can empathize with Job as he wrestled with his understanding of God and the futility of life.

In the middle of suffering, the only thing that we may be able to hold on to is a declaration. While Job could not comprehend his suffering or God's ways, he knew in his heart and declared with his lips, "My Redeemer lives." Be uplifted as you dwell on that declaration. God is the one that ultimately has the final say for your life and for this earth, and you can boldly claim that he lives!

Lord God, thank you for the men and women who walked on this earth before us, who demonstrated astounding faith in the midst of suffering. I declare now, Lord, throughout the troubles of life, that my Redeemer lives!

Contentment

I know what it is to be in need, and I know what it is to have plenty.
I have learned the secret of being content in any and every situation,
whether well fed or hungry, whether living in plenty or in want.

PHILIPPIANS 4:12 NIV

What is the secret that Paul understood about contentment, and why
would you need it in times of plenty? The shortcoming of both poverty and
riches is that we always want more.

The secret to Paul's contentment was that he had experienced God's
provision of his spiritual, emotional, and physical needs and knew that he
didn't need anything more than trust in the Lord Jesus Christ. You don't
need more to make you happy. Jesus is more than enough for you. Once
you understand that, you can say, like Paul, that you have learned the secret
of being content.

Dear Lord, please forgive me for carrying an attitude of always
wanting more. I know that you have given me everything that I need
and that you are taking care of me. I pray for contentment in my
heart as I trust you in all things.

Search Me

Search me, O God, and know my heart;
Try me and know my anxious thoughts;
And see if there be any hurtful way in me,
And lead me in the everlasting way.

PSALM 139:23-24 NASB

Searching requires looking in every place available to
see what is there. Asking God to search your heart means that you are
inviting him to know everything that is in it. Vulnerability is hard, particularly
when we are battling pride or when we want to hide painful feelings or
even sin.

Of course, God already knows your heart, so there is no point in hiding from
him. But when you invite him in, you are acknowledging that you might
need him to show you things in your heart and mind that need his love and
guidance. Know that as you surrender to him, his love will cover all wrong,
and he will lead you in the everlasting way.

Search me, O God, and know my heart.
Help me to put aside my anxious thoughts and hurtful ways.
I want to be led in your everlasting way.

DAY 229

Returned Love

I love those who love me,
and those who seek me find me.
PROVERBS 8:17 NIV

With God, we never have to worry about being the one who bestows unrequited love. We always know, with absolute certainty, that our love—no matter how passionate—is even more passionately returned. God loves those who love him; he wants to be sought by you. But even more than that, he longs to be found by you.

Don't think that when you cry out to him you're speaking to thin air. He hears you and loves you. He gives himself to you. Continue in your love for him. Continue in your pursuit of him. He will give himself to you with even greater abandon than you can imagine.

Jesus, thank you for loving me perfectly. Thank you for giving yourself to me fully. Thank you that you have made a way for me to enter your glory and to be loved by you forever.

DAY 230

Continual Praise

From the rising of the sun to its going down
The LORD's name is to be praised.

PSALM 113:3 NKJV

What would it look like to be people who praise God from the time we awaken each morning until the time we fall asleep each night? Not only would we be pleasing God as we worship him constantly, but we would also effect an incredible change in our personal outlook.

Intentional, continual praise can only naturally result in intentional, continual joy. When we choose to look at each moment as a moment in which to be thankful and worshipful, then we will find in each moment beauty, joy, and satisfaction.

Lord, I praise you for your love for me. I pray that you would help me to be one who praises you all day, every day. I pray that you would cultivate in me an appreciation of your goodness and a longing to worship you constantly.

DAY 231

Gracious

Yet the LORD longs to be gracious to you;
therefore he will rise up to show you compassion.
For the LORD is a God of justice.
Blessed are all who wait for him!

ISAIAH 30:18 NIV

We can become so overwhelmed by our own shame, troubles, or misconceptions that we miss out on the most simple and beautiful truth— our God greatly desires to show us grace. He doesn't long to show us his anger or his punishment. He doesn't rise up to show us his power and his terrible greatness; he rises up to show us compassion.

When we enter God's presence with this point of view, we are humbled by his love despite his justice—because the punishment we deserve has been outweighed by the grace he longs to give.

I am humbled by the power of your grace for me. Help me to wait for you and to always rely on your grace and your compassion more than my own strength and capacity for goodness.

DAY 232

Full Joy

"So you have pain now; but I will see you again,
and your hearts will rejoice, and no one will
take your joy from you."

JOHN 16:22 NRSV

The joy that comes with the presence of the Lord is a joy that cannot be taken away. When we remember what Christ has done for us, and think about how his grace has changed the eternal course of our lives, we cannot help but be filled with an irrepressible joy.

We may struggle on difficult days, when our lives get hard, to keep sight of the joy of our salvation. But a day is coming when Jesus will return to this earth—setting all things right—and on that day, we will experience our joy in full.

Thank you, Jesus, for the joy of my salvation. Thank you that, in your presence, my joy cannot be taken away from me. I look forward to the day when I will see you face to face, in fullness of joy.

Kept in the Race

"Do not be afraid; you have done all this evil. Yet do not turn aside from following the LORD, but serve the LORD with all your heart."

1 SAMUEL 12:20 ESV

We often struggle, thinking we need to forgive ourselves because we lack peace about the sins of our past. The fact of the matter is this: Jesus' forgiveness is what is important, and if Jesus sets you free, you have no opinion in the matter any longer. Jesus forgave your sins. He brushes the dirt off your knees, kissing and bandaging your wounds. Now you can run again.

In running, never stop for the sake of hopelessness or doubt. Never take your hand off the plow because you feel unworthy. You never earned the right to serve God. Jesus is the one who bought you, and he is the one who forgave you. If the one who will judge all things has declared you clean, then you are a bride who is spotless.

God, help me to serve you with all my heart. Free me from condemnation and grief. Help me to truly know your love and forgiveness. Thank you for redeeming me and drawing me to you.

DAY 234

Wholly Devoted

*He alone is your God, the only one who is worthy of your praise,
the one who has done these mighty miracles that you have
seen with your own eyes.*

DEUTERONOMY 10:21 NLT

At the unveiling of the city's newest skyscraper, crowds gather to celebrate the feat of architecture and engineering, commerce and creativity. Sunlight pours onto the observation deck as a city official cuts the yellow dedication ribbon. Behind him are some of the many construction workers, designers, and engineers whose imagination, insight, and expertise contributed to making mere drawings a reality. But only one expert—the architect— can truly take credit for the building's inception. He intimately knows it. Everyone around him reaches for the spotlight, and the architect is lost in the noise and clamor for glory.

You know this architect. He is your designer: the one responsible for your soaring heights and multitude of blessings. *He alone is your God.* Have you singled him out for glory? *The only one who is worthy of your praise.* Have you heralded to him a song of thanksgiving? The mighty miracles of your life are his careful design, plain for all to see.

*God, I want to be wholly devoted to you, the architect
of my life. You know me inside and out. Thank you
for your hand of blessing. I give you the glory and
honor for all you have done in my life.*

Encouragement in the Word

I wait for your deliverance, O Lord,
for your words thrill me like nothing else!
Invigorate my life so that I can praise you even more,
and may your truth be my strength!

PSALM 119:174-175 TPT

There is wonder to be found in snowflakes, raindrops, and even strange bugs. Though we often don't love the idea of encountering too many of those things, if we stop and look, if we allow ourselves to really *see* what is there, it's pretty amazing.

The same can be true of God's Word. It may be displayed in various forms and places throughout our homes, schools, work places, or church buildings, but if we don't stop to really drink in the words that are there, we can miss the rich blessing behind them. When we believe that God wants to encourage us through his Word, we will no doubt find encouragement in it—because God intended it to be used for that purpose!

Don't gloss over the beauty and depth of his Word. It's the only Word that carries the richness of eternity.

God, help me not to gloss over the beauty and depth of your Word. Only your Word carries the richness of eternity and the encouragement I need for each new day.

Enduring Hardship

Let perseverance finish its work so that you may be
mature and complete, not lacking anything.
JAMES 1:4 NIV

Creating a diamond is, for the transforming coal, a long and painful process.
Simple carbon undergoes an immense refining pressure that produces
a wholly new creation. We might just see a cloudy rock at this stage, but
there is another refining step to be taken. After the stone-cutter does his
work, a precise shining diamond emerges: magnificent, glittering, brilliant.

When we endure hardship, the long and painful process can seem unfair.
But our life stories are written by a compassionate Creator who is crafting
a masterpiece. He is refining us, like the diamond, into something entirely
beyond our imagination. And we can rejoice in the beauty he is creating.
You may not see it now, but it's coming soon.

*Father, show me the emerging beauty under the surface of the
hardships I face. I submit to your process and trust your skilled and
loving hands. Let me come out of this situation stronger
and brighter, shining for you.*

DAY 237

Eternity

We are citizens of heaven, where the Lord Jesus Christ lives. And we are
eagerly waiting for him to return as our Savior.

PHILIPPIANS 3:20 NLT

The question of eternity is a heavy one. The Bible tells us that heaven is
a real place, inhabited by those who have accepted Jesus Christ as their
Savior. Those who haven't trusted him will spend eternity alienated from
him, which is the essence of hell: an eternity absent of anything good. But
believers in Jesus' death and resurrection for the forgiveness of sins will live
and share in his glory. Our bodies will be transformed and everything will
come under his control.

What a relief to know the truth! Eternity is a guarantee, and yours can
be one of heavenly citizenship. You have been promised an inheritance
of glory, where all pain, suffering, and weakness will be transformed. All
deception, hatred, and greed will come under the control of Jesus Christ
as he makes all things new. By faith, your eternity is established.

*Father, thank you for the hope of an eternity spent with you and the
rest of your children. How wonderful it will be to share in your glory
and watch all things become new.*

Where He Leads Me

With weeping they shall come,
and with pleas for mercy I will lead them back,
I will make them walk by brooks of water,
in a straight path in which they shall not stumble,
for I am a father to Israel.

JEREMIAH 31:9 ESV

The journey of the believer is a lifelong pilgrimage that ends not at a religious temple or city, but in the kingdom of heaven. Our journey's hardships, sacrifices, and struggles are part of our displacement, and they won't end until eternity. Wherever the path leads, we follow. However long and dusty the road, we press on. No matter what storms lay ahead, we continue. With determined steps we press on toward our destination until we are welcomed home.

The many steps of our pilgrimage are not walked alone, but alongside one who never gets lost, tired, or afraid. He knows we are confused and alone, so he personally leads us. He knows we are thirsty, so he refreshes us along the way. He knows we are bruised and broken, so he navigates a straight route for our safety. He is a good Father and we can trust his leadership. Your pilgrimage is a long and beautiful journey, and it's worth every step.

Lord, wherever you lead me in this season, I trust you enough to say that I will follow. I believe that you know the best path for me, and you will not leave me to find my way alone.

Garment of Praise

Enter his gates with thanksgiving,
and his courts with praise.
Give thanks to him, bless his name.
For the LORD is good;
his steadfast love endures forever,
and his faithfulness to all generations.

PSALM 100:4-5 NRSV

Have you ever looked into a child's grumpy face and demanded that they don't smile? Even the most stubborn child can often be coaxed out of their funk by a few tickles or funny faces. Unfortunately, the same can't be said for adults. Imagine trying to change the attitude of a crotchety older woman with the same method. The picture is somewhat ridiculous.

When life's situations get us down, and all around us is darkness and depression, it takes a great deal of faith to choose praise. But often that's the only thing that can really pull us out of those dark moments. When we choose to thank God for his goodness and grace, we can't help but see life in a more positive light. As we praise God, our focus shifts from ourselves to him.

God, you don't only deserve my praise when life is going well. You are worthy of my adoration every second of every day—no matter what the situation. Today I choose to put on a garment of praise.

Every Word

In the same way the Spirit also helps our weakness; for we do not know how to pray as we should, but the Spirit Himself intercedes for us with groanings too deep for words; and He who searches the hearts knows what the mind of the Spirit is, because He intercedes for the saints according to the will of God.

ROMANS 8:26-27 NASB

When we are too weak in our flesh to know how or what to pray, we can count on the Holy Spirit to show us the way. What a relief! When the words don't seem to come out right or our supplications feel empty, we can submit to the Holy Spirit to intercede for us with prayers beyond mere words.

God hears his children. And he hears his Spirit in a language that only the holy can utter. Believe that God hears your prayers. The Holy Spirit in you will never run out of things to say to the Father. Cry out, however you can, and know that he hears every word.

God, thank you for listening to my every word.
Holy Spirit, thank you for talking to the Father when I can't get the words out. I choose to believe that my words matter to you.

The Protection of God

For You have been a defense for the helpless,
a defense for the needy in his distress,
a refuge from the storm, a shade from the heat.

ISAIAH 25:4 NASB

In Christ, we are protected. We have a strong shield, a faithful defender, and a constant guardian. Many have mistaken this promise as a guarantee against pain, suffering, or hardship. When sorrows overwhelm us, can we stay faithful to our protector? Will we interpret adversity as betrayal, or embrace a protection that sometimes involves endurance?

God's security shelters us according to what we need, not necessarily from what pains us. The storms will rage and the heat will blister, each in their turn and maybe for a long time. Can you believe that he is protecting you through it all? His hand is upon you, defending and sheltering you; let no storm shake your faith in this, beloved.

Father, I believe your hand of protection is over
my life even when things aren't going as I hope.
My faith is deepened when I recognize that
you are with me in the storm.

A Specific Purpose

We are God's handiwork, created in Christ Jesus to do good works,
which God prepared in advance for us to do.

EPHESIANS 2:10 NIV

Very few people know exactly what they want to be *when they grow up*. We take multiple tests to find out our personality types, strengths, and spiritual gifts, all to determine what we should do with our lives. While these tests can be good indicators of suitable opportunities, the best way to find the perfect fit is to go directly to the source.

No matter what you may have been told, you were planned by God. That means he put you on this earth for a very specific reason. God's desire is that you will partner with him in that plan. When you begin to walk in his purpose, you will find the joy, peace, strength, and grace you need to carry it out.

I choose to believe that you, God, have a purpose for my life. I don't want to limit you with my plans and desires because you have something bigger and better for me to do than I can even imagine. I pray you will begin to reveal it to me now.

Everything I Do

Let us not grow weary of doing good, for in due season we will reap,
if we do not give up.
GALATIANS 6:9 ESV

"Look at me! Look at me! Watch this!" Oh how often children seek recognition from just about anyone who will watch. Even though the dive bomb into the water looks exactly the same as it did last time, or the cartwheel is still lopsided after thirty attempts, onlookers continue to encourage the repetitious behavior. Are we really very different from those children? Don't we also look for recognition in life? We want someone to notice our efforts, our charity, our diligence, our excellence. And, though we hate to admit it, we may even get a little upset if nobody does.

We can choose to search for recognition from others, or we can believe that God sees everything we do. Because he does. He is interested in that project we worked so hard on. He is delighted when we spend our time serving others. He loves it when we do our very best.

God, I don't want to waste my time trying to be recognized by others. I want to share what I have without holding back, knowing that you have your eye on me and you don't look away.

Remember God's Faithfulness

Those who love me, I will deliver;
I will protect those who know my name.
When they call to me, I will answer them;
I will be with them in trouble,
I will rescue them and honor them.

PSALM 91:14-15 NRSV

When we read God's Word, we glue our need to God's provision. We read the words on the page and realize God has helped people with the same needs as ours. Whether it's for love or wisdom, provision or righteousness, Jesus has all we need. He is a generous giver, and he has beckoned us closer to receive what he has for us—including intimacy with him.

Read through his Word and be trained of him. Let the Holy Spirit teach you all things as you ponder and reflect. Read the Psalms for comfort and encouragement; study the Proverbs for deeper wisdom. God's Word is written for you, and it belongs to you.

Lord, please help me read your Word and understand it the way you intend. I trust you to grow my faith and meet my needs as I learn and profit from your wisdom. I love you!

Strength Every Morning

LORD, be gracious to us;
we long for you.
Be our strength every morning,
our salvation in time of distress.

ISAIAH 33:2 NIV

In times of crisis, each new morning demands our strength. In seasons of difficulty, waking brings with it worry, fear, and distress. We all look for strength in different places; some of us find security in financial wellness, others in physical health, still others in community and friendships.

If Christ is the ultimate source of strength, then each new morning we will open his Word and find truth to counteract worry with peace, fear with understanding, and distress with steadfastness. His grace will make us more than able to rise each morning with strength for the day.

I need your strength, Lord, to face the hardships in my life. Each new morning I want to run to your presence so that I can be filled by your spirit and made ready in your love.

A Basket Case

> "I took the load off their shoulders;
> I let them put down their baskets."
>
> PSALM 81:6 NCV

People in developing countries typically have few options when a heavy load of some kind must be moved. In Africa, a tribal woman can carry up to 70% of her body weight on the top of her head. Physical burdens are—yes—burdensome and require strength and stamina.

Spiritual and emotional burdens are the same. The heaviness and fatigue of the soul can bring depression and even a loss of hope. There is great news, however! We have a burden bearer—one who is well equipped and ready to remove our hands from our heavy load! Our responsibility is to let him do it. Put all of your concerns, worries, fears, and doubts into God's mighty basket and let him haul it away! You don't have to be a basket case!

Lord, today I'm placing all of my concerns into your ample basket. I release it to your care. As you solve all these issues, let me know how to proceed one step at a time. Thank you for being my burden bearer!

Are You Shining

"You are the light of the world.
A city set on a hill cannot be hidden."
MATTHEW 5:14 ESV

Lights from major cities like Los Angeles, Nashville, and Atlanta can be seen from space. In fact, their brilliance increases 50% more during the holiday season! These cities simply cannot be hidden.

As believers, we are to be a light, shining for all to see. If there ever was a time in history where the beacon of light needed to illumine the darkness, it is now! We dare not hide behind the façade of political correctness and fear, but rather speak and live in the luminance of Christ's truth. We have the light of the world living in us and we know the truth that sets us free.

*Lord, shine through me this day. Give me courage
to speak and live according to your Word, no matter what
the world may say. I want your glow to radiate through me.*

DAY 248

Bad News

They will have no fear of bad news;
their hearts are steadfast, trusting in the LORD.
PSALM 112:7 NIV

In this age of technology, we can be inundated with happenings from around the word. News is always at our fingertips—and often it's not good. Sometimes we are waiting for the personal, life-changing kind of news: the medical report, the upshot of the job interview, the test score. Our fear is that the result will not be what we hope.

Psalm 112 tells us that we do not have to fear bad news! If our hearts are righteous, we are steadfast and secure. In spite of any alarming information coming our way, we can be at peace because we are safe in God's hands.

I am so thankful, Lord, that even though bad news assaults and sometimes awaits, I do not need to fear even the scariest of prospects. I am safe and secure in you no matter the situation.

Bloom

"They are those who, hearing the word, hold it fast in an
honest and good heart, and bear fruit with patience."

LUKE 8:15 ESV

Most of us want to make a significant mark somewhere in our lifetime.
It's comforting to believe that the routine of our ordinary lives is merely
preparation for the really big assignment that surely is just around the
corner. You know, the lofty thing, the high calling, the noble assignment
that undoubtedly is directly ahead.

Then one day in a moment of quiet, the Lord whispers, "This is it. What you
are doing is what I've called you to do. Do your work, love your neighbor,
serve people, seek me first, and everything in your heart you long for will be
fulfilled. Be faithful right where I've put you. You don't need to accomplish
great things for me. Just be."

*Lord, I so long for significance. I want my life to matter.
Help me to understand that it's not what I do for you that is
important, it's whose I am and who I am. Help me to be faithful
in the assignment you have given me right now.*

Blackbird Bluff

Stay alert! Watch out for your great enemy, the devil. He prowls around like a roaring lion, looking for someone to devour. Stand firm against him, and be strong in your faith.

1 PETER 5:8-9 NLT

In the parking lot of a lovely little park, a sleek blackbird demanded attention. He was busy pecking at a small wad of bread, surely enjoying an unexpected treat. A much larger blackbird circled him menacingly—moving in closer, then hopping back. The smaller bird seemed completely oblivious. He was not in the least frightened, and he continued to enjoy his dinner. After a moment, the bully bird backed off. He was suddenly the same size as the other bird. He had puffed his feathers out in an attempt to look big and scary. The smaller bird knew he was a phony and paid him no mind.

The Bible describes our enemy, Satan, as a roaring lion, prowling around looking for someone to devour. A lion that roars is not to be feared because he has given his presence away, allowing his prey time to escape. When we are in tune with God, we don't need to fear Satan's tactics. Satan's roar is not to be feared because compared to God he is all blackbird bluff. Let's pay him no mind!

Lord, give me discernment so that I can recognize the enemy's tactics and lies. Thank you for giving me the victory as I take my stand against his wiles.

Bridging the Gap

Faith is the confidence that what we hope
for will actually happen; it gives us assurance
about things we cannot see.

HEBREWS 11:1 NLT

Do you ever feel like there is an enormous gap between what you *know*
to be true in God's Word and what you *feel* to be true? Our feelings
are so fickle. They fluctuate depending on our circumstances, much as
our moods change with the weather. The good news is that they don't
change facts! God promises strength, wisdom, peace, hope, direction,
comfort, forgiveness, courage, eternal life, and so much more. These are
unchangeable—they are written in stone.

How do we move from the tyranny of emotions to the confidence of faith?
We must determine to believe what God says instead of what our emotions
say, and then declare his promises aloud! Then we do it again and again and
again until faith rises and bridges the gap.

*Lord, your Word is true and I know it. Right now,
I feel so alone and frightened even though I know
you promise never to leave me or forsake me.
I choose to believe the truth. Help me now by the
power of your Spirit.*

Clay Pots

You, LORD, are our Father.
We are the clay, you are the potter;
we are all the work of your hand.
ISAIAH 64:8 NIV

There are many types of pottery—from basic earthenware used for mundane tasks to lovely, decorative pieces that adorn someone's mantelpiece. It is interesting to note that God uses this imagery all the way from Genesis to Revelation. He is the potter; we are the clay. The potter has absolute power to create exactly according to his wish; the pot has no say.

There are times when we are not happy with the vessel the potter has fashioned. We'd rather be the vase on the mantelpiece that is used to hold a beautiful bouquet. The truth is, the vessel itself is not what gives it worth—as beautiful as it may be. The value lies in the contents.

Lord, forgive me for being discontented with this vessel you created. I know that outward appearance is meaningless compared to the inward glory of Christ's presence. Shine through this vessel; use me as you wish, and let the world know who you are.

Held Together

He is before all things,
and in him all things hold together.
COLOSSIANS 1:17 NIV

Often life seems to be a conglomeration of unrelated activities and we feel pulled in a thousand directions simultaneously. Loose ends, unfinished business, and to-do lists leave us feeling a day late and a dollar short. Frustration, discouragement, and anxiety often overwhelm. The apostle Paul must have experienced something similar when he was on a ship headed to Jerusalem to be tried in court. An enormous storm raged. In an effort to survive, the sailors wrapped ropes around the body of the ship to keep it from falling apart. God promised Paul that all would survive the wreck, and they did!

What an amazing truth it is to know that it is not our job to hold our lives together. Our responsibility is to submit our to-do list to God, bow to his will, and let him hold it all together. He is the rope that holds us fast.

Lord, thank you that you are the glue that keeps me together. Today as I face the impossible list of my responsibilities, I submit to your will and ask you to hold everything in place.

DAY 254

Joy

Do not grieve, for the joy of the LORD is your strength.
NEHEMIAH 8:10 NIV

Joy is not necessarily happiness. Happiness is dependent on circumstances; joy is not. Happiness is fleeting; joy is constant. Happiness disappears when trials come; joy grows through troubles. Good times bring happiness and laughter; difficulties bring sorrow and grief, but joy resides beneath.

Joy is not an emotion that can be fabricated or faked. It is a deep-seated sense that all things are well because God is in charge. Joy is expressed in praise, song, laughter, a peaceful countenance, a light in the eyes, or a serenity that belies any adversity. It is the substance of the soul that holds us together as we trust in God, who does all things well. Jesus wants our joy to be full!

Thank you, Jesus, for the joy that gives me strength. I choose today to fill my mind with truth, to think about those things that are praiseworthy, and to trust you fully. With a thankful heart, I choose joy.

Fear

Fear and intimidation is a trap that holds you back.
But when you place your confidence in the Lord,
you will be seated in the high place.

PROVERBS 29:25 TPT

If you live in America, it is impossible not to look at today's date and remember—whether from experience or from hearing about it over the years—one of the darkest days in our history. Thousands of lives were lost in a well-planned terrorist attack, and in many ways, things were never again the same. Air travel, for example, continues to evoke a spirit of fear in many hearts that was previously unimagined.

In the New Living Translation alone, the word *fear* appears 601 times. Primarily, it is there to remind us to fear God; in doing so, he will abate all other fears. The fear God desires from us is not one of mistrust, but one of respect and awe. If we believe completely in his sovereign power, if we give him all our reverence, how can we fear anything else? If God is for us, there is truly nothing to fear. Hallelujah!

*Lord, I lay my fear at your feet today, and I place my trust in you.
I know that no matter what my circumstance may be,
my safety in you is secure.*

The End of the Tunnel

"I am the light of the world. Whoever follows me will never walk in darkness, but will have the light of life."

JOHN 8:12 NIV

There's an old adage dating back to the 1800s we've probably all quoted: "There is a light at the end of the tunnel." Translated: "Hang on. The end of whatever difficulty you are in is in sight!" However, there are times when there probably is no positive ending to be had, and there is no light at the end of our tunnel. What then?

Jesus is light and he dwells in us. We are surrounded by his presence no matter where we are. He is behind us, before us, to the right and the left, above and beneath. We are cocooned in his presence and do not walk in darkness. He is our light. No more walking through dark tunnels with only a spot of hope at the end. We walk through our tunnels blazing with the light of Jesus!

Lord, I acknowledge that you, the light of the world, live in me. I do not need to fear the darkness or the outcome. Help me remember that the light of your presence never leaves me.

Starting Over

Praise the LORD!
Oh, give thanks to the LORD, for He is good!
For His mercy endures forever.
PSALM 106:1 NKJV

Have you ever wished you could have a do-over? It would be so great to turn back the clock, reverse a decision, and do it differently. There is so much more wisdom in looking back! Yes, there are some things we can do over, like tweak the recipe or rip the seam, but most often, the important big decisions can't be changed.

Except when it comes to spiritual things. God tells us that we can start over every morning because his mercies will be there. Whatever went awry the day before, whatever mess we made from poor choices, we can begin the next day with a completely clean slate! There does not need to be any carryover of yesterday's mistakes. Our part in the transaction may require repentance of sin or forgiving someone, perhaps even ourselves. Bathed in his mercies, we can begin each day squeaky clean!

Lord, I am so grateful that your love and your mercies never end. You extend them to me brand new every morning!
Great is your faithfulness!

Waiting

Wait for the LORD;
Be strong, and let your heart take courage;
Yes, wait for the LORD!
PSALM 27:14 NASB

Is there anything positive to be said about waiting? Whether we are in line at the grocery store, stuck in traffic, or simply waiting for a package to arrive, it is part of our daily lives. Waiting seems like a colossal waste of time. And yet, God tells us specifically (35 times or so) we are to "wait for the Lord."

The concept of waiting on God seems to originate with the Psalmist. Perhaps it was because he was so often stuck in perilous situations and he knew his only hope was God. The kind of waiting he speaks of is not passive as though our spiritual lives are put on hold until God comes through with our request. It is an active display of faith as we lay down our desires, hopes, and dreams before the Lord and surrender to his will. In the waiting, he is perfecting our faith and building our character.

Oh Lord, how I loathe waiting. I am so impatient. God grant me the grace to humbly wait upon you as you conform me to your image. Your timing is best and I surrender to it.

Songs of Victory

You are my hiding place;
you protect me from trouble.
You surround me with songs of victory.

PSALM 32:7 NLT

Life can feel like a battle sometimes. From keeping up with busy schedules to making major decisions, we are met with challenges daily. Some days we just want to hide away for a while so we can recharge and refocus.

God is our hiding place—our protection and our rest. He walks with us through the battles of life and sings a song of victory over us. With Christ as our strength, we can not only make it through the battle, but we can come out as joyful victors.

Lord, as I face the challenges in my daily life, help me run to you. As I hide myself in you, give me your peace, your rest, and your hope. I pray that I would enter my battles with confidence, knowing that you will give me the victory.

The Questioning Soul

Trust in him at all times, you people;
pour out your hearts to him,
for God is our refuge.

PSALM 62:8 NIV

There are questions that we long to have answered by God, and circumstances in our lives that leave us wondering about his goodness. As we pray, we try to rend the heavens for an answer that will make sense of our storm.

What God desires most isn't the soul with the answer—it's the one laid bare before him in a perfect dance of trust, belief, and raw vulnerability. In that moment of emptiness before your Maker, he will be your safe place. Pour out your heart to him and rest in his embrace because he is a refuge for even the most questioning soul.

God, I don't have answers for all of the deep questions, but I know that you are a safe place for me to pour out my heart. I give you my questions and my fears, and I say yes to the peace of your presence.

Stronghold

The LORD is good,
A stronghold in the day of trouble;
And He knows those who trust in Him.

NAHUM 1:7 NKJV

God isn't only with us when our faith comes easy and our praise is unrestrained. Even in the day of trouble, God knows intimately those who trust him, and he is a stronghold for them.

Not only in catastrophe, but even in our moments of hidden weakness, God is our strength and our refuge. We can trust him and know that he is always good.

Thank you, Lord, that you are a source of strength for me even in my weakest moments. You remember my trust in you when I feel close to losing my faith. You do not forget me, and you are more than enough for me. You take my darkest hour and bring the light of your countenance to me.

Most Beautiful of All

Here's the one thing I crave from God,
the one thing I seek above all else:
I want the privilege of living with him
every moment in his house,
finding the sweet loveliness of his face,
filled with awe, delighting in his glory and grace.
I want to live my life so close to him
that he takes pleasure in my every prayer.

PSALM 27:4 TPT

If there is one thing that we can appreciate, it's something pretty. Shiny things easily catch our attention, and we seek to surround ourselves with beauty. There is much beauty to be found in our natural world.

There is nothing wrong with finding *loveliness* in our world, but if there is one thing that is more beautiful than anything else, it is the Lord God himself. His love, his mercy, his grace, and his understanding—it is nothing short of breathtaking.

Lord, I don't want to miss your beauty today. I seek after it because I know it can be found. You created me to enjoy all that is exquisite, beautiful, and captivating—and that is you! Nothing is better than you and your love.

Chorus of Love

"The LORD your God is with you,
the Mighty Warrior who saves.
He will take great delight in you;
in his love he will no longer rebuke you,
but will rejoice over you with singing."

ZEPHANIAH 3:17 NIV

Oh, the many ways in which we sin! We are full of mistakes. We make so many poor choices. The list of ways in which we fall short is endless.

If we are truly repentant, we don't need to spend time beating ourselves up over the mistakes we make. We get to say we're sorry and then move on. Scripture tells us that the Lord takes great delight in us! When Jesus died to save us from our sins, there was no longer need for rebuke. Instead, he rejoices over us with singing! Can you imagine? The very God who saved us is so thrilled about it that he sings us a song.

Lord, thank you for the chorus you sing over me.
The very fact that I exist gives you great pleasure.
I repent of my sin, and rejoice with you today!

DAY 264

Safety Guaranteed

You will be guarded by God himself.
You will be safe when you leave your home
and safely you will return.
He will protect you now,
and he'll protect you forevermore!

PSALM 121:7-8 TPT

Huddled in the basement of the museum, visitors waited for the hurricane to pass. Children cried or slept; parents' expressions were tight and anxious. Museum staff held walkie-talkies and flashlights, beams bouncing nervously. Sirens wailed, winds howled, and the depths of the shelter shook as the mighty storm raged outside.

Even with modern engineering advancements implemented, those sheltered from the storm were worried. There was no guarantee of safety. Could we expect the huddled crowds to be singing for joy? Rejoicing in their place of refuge? If they were aware of the one who has promised to always protect, then their praises would echo off the shelter walls!

In the shadow of your protection, God, I can be glad. You are the only one able to guarantee my safety! Your protection spreads over me, stronger than any bomb shelter or apocalyptic bunker that could ever be built. With you, I can delight through the storm.

Never-ending Joy

My heart rejoices in the LORD!
The LORD has made me strong.
Now I have an answer for my enemies;
I rejoice because you rescued me.
No one is holy like the LORD!
There is no one besides you;
there is no Rock like our God.

1 SAMUEL 2:1-2 NLT

Consider for a moment the most joyous time of your walk with Christ. Imagine the delight of that season, the lightness and pleasure in your heart. Rest in the memory for a minute, and let the emotions come back to you. Is the joy returning? Do you feel it? Now, hear this truth: The way you felt about God at the highest, most joyful, amazing, glorious moment is how he feels about you at all times!

What a glorious blessing! Our joy is an overflow of his heart's joy toward us; it is just one of the many blessings God showers over us. When we realize how good he is, and that he has granted us everything we need for salvation through Jesus, we can rejoice!

Thank you , Lord, that the season of my greatest rejoicing can be now—when I consider the strength you provide, the suffering from which I have been rescued, and the rock that is you.

Embracing Weakness

Humble yourselves in the sight of the Lord,
and He will lift you up.
JAMES 4:10 NKJV

Do you ever find yourself suddenly aware of your own glaring weaknesses? Aware that, if left up to your own good works, you wouldn't stand a chance of attaining salvation? We should find great comfort in the fact that we are nothing without salvation in Christ Jesus.

Thankfully, God made a way for us to be united with him, despite impatience, selfishness, anger, and pride. God deeply cares for us and patiently sustains us with steady, faithful, and adoring love. Amazingly, his love even goes beyond this to *embrace* and *transform* our weakness when we yield it to him. Weakness isn't something to be feared or hidden; weakness submitted to God allows the power of Christ to work in and through us.

God, knowing my weakness makes me more aware of my need for your strength. I humbly ask you to be strong where I am weak. Thank you that your transformative love is waiting to graciously restore me.

A Worthy Friend

Let all that I am praise the LORD;
may I never forget the good things he does for me.
He forgives all my sins and heals all my diseases.
He redeems me from death and crowns me
with love and tender mercies.
He fills my life with good things.
My youth is renewed like the eagle's!

PSALM 103:2-5 NLT

God created us for relationship with him. He loves to spend time with us whether we're freshly showered or barely awake in our wrinkled pajamas. It doesn't matter to him if our teeth are brushed, bed is made, and laundry is put away. He takes us just as we are.

There aren't many friends in life who could say the same. There are few we would allow into our homes if we weren't yet "ready for the day." That's why God is the very best friend. He loves us just as we are; he will sit and listen to us regardless of our state.

God, you really are the best friend I have. Thank you for listening intently to me even when I whine or have stinky morning breath. I treasure your friendship.

DAY 268

The Plan

By faith Abraham, when called to go to a place he would
later receive as his inheritance, obeyed and went,
even though he did not know where he was going.

HEBREWS 11:8 NIV

We all like to have a map laid out for us to see every bend and every turn
in the road. As Christians, we spend so much of our time searching for the
"will of God." Oftentimes when it comes to the will of God, we can, quite
honestly, just miss the point. We look for what God wants us to do, but we
miss out on seeing who he is.

We aren't always going to know where we're headed. But the heart of God
is for us to know *him*. Not to know every detail of the plan. Not to know
what someone else's story is. Just to know him for who he is. The closer
you are to God, the more delighted in you he will be. And isn't that our
longing? For God to delight in us?

*Jesus, help me abide in you so you can truly accomplish your perfect
will in me. I come before you today stripped of questions and my
need to know the plan. I just need to know you.*

The Power of Seeking

Even there you can look for the LORD your God,
and you will find him if you look for him with your whole being.

DEUTERONOMY 4:29 NCV

Do you have days when you feel empty, weary, and uninspired? Days when you feel you have nothing to give, even though there is no shortage of demand. You don't know how to fill back up; you only know that you need to.

The Lord says that if you look for him with your whole being, you will find him. God will not withhold himself from his child who asks. Even here, in this place of emptiness, you can be filled—you just have to seek.

God, I am sitting here before you asking you to fill me. I don't have the words for an eloquent prayer, or the equipping for great faith, but I do have the heart to be filled by you. Show yourself to me today.

DAY 270

Worthy

"You are worthy, O Lord,
To receive glory and honor and power;
For You created all things,
And by Your will they exist and were created."
REVELATION 4:11 NKJV

Worship is our natural response to the goodness of God. It's not simply an emotional reaction—worship is also the act of offering back to God the glory that he rightly deserves. When we stop to think about God's power, majesty, and creativity, we cannot help but glorify him because he is so worthy of the highest form of honor.

By glorifying God in our daily lives, those around us will take notice and some will ultimately be led to join us in praising him.

God help me to praise you in the way that you are worthy of.
Help me to respond to you with honor, appreciation, and worship.
I want to look for you in everything, so I can give praise back
to you for all you've done.

Your Eyes Will See

Your eyes will see the King in His beauty;
They will behold a far-distant land.

ISAIAH 33:17 NASB

On the difficult days when our faith is weak, our tears flow freely, and our hearts are discouraged, we wish just to see God. We think that if we could look into his eyes, have the chance to ask him our deepest questions—and hear them answered—then we could continue on.

Beloved, the reality of heaven is closer than we can imagine. We will see our King, in all his greatness and his beauty. We will look upon that distant land of heaven. We will one day dwell there in peace: with every question answered and every tear dried.

Thank you, God, that you have promised heaven to me through my belief in your Son. Thank you that I will see your face one day and walk with you in your kingdom. When the days are hard, help me to remember that in just a little while all will be well and I will be with you.

DAY 272

Unhindered

Because of Christ and our faith in him, we can now
come boldly and confidently into God's presence.

EPHESIANS 3:12 NLT

Our salvation awards us the great privilege of being able to approach God
unhindered. With sin no longer dividing us from his holy presence, we are
free to bare our souls to God as his beloved sons and daughters.

As bold and confident lovers of God, there is nothing we cannot share
with him—and he with us. Fear and shame have no place in this kind of
excellent love.

*I love you, Lord. I praise you that you made a way for me to love you
unhindered. I don't want my fear and my shame to interrupt our
relationship—so I ask you to take it from me. Show me what
it means to be a bold and confident child of yours.*

Fulfilling God's Dreams

Only let each person lead the life that the Lord has assigned to him,
and to which God has called him. This is my rule in all the churches.

1 CORINTHIANS 7:17 ESV

God created you perfectly to be the person he planned for you to be. He
has plans for your life and purposes for your talents. When we long to be
someone else, or somewhere else, we miss out on the incredible plan that
God has for who we are right where we are.

By devoting ourselves to live the life we've been called to, we fulfill God's
excellent dream for our lives. There is no greater privilege than to honor
our Creator by living out the purpose he planned for us.

*Lord, I want to bring you honor in the way that I live
and glory in how I use my unique talents. Make your calling
clear to me so that I can fulfill it.*

Found in a Desert

He found them in a desert,
a windy, empty land.
He surrounded them and brought them up,
guarding them as those he loved very much.

DEUTERONOMY 32:10 NCV

Do you ever go through seasons in your life where you just feel dark? Perhaps directionless or uninspired? In a metaphorical wilderness where you can't get a glimpse of any vision or even hope, God can find you. Even in the deserts of your own heart where you can't muster the strength to reach out to him, he can and will meet you.

Wait for the Lord, even in your emptiness; wait for him and he will come for you.

Thank you, Father, that you are near to me even when my heart is broken and my strength has failed. Thank you that you find me in my wilderness and you will restore me to joy.

Never Wasted

Now may our Lord Jesus Christ himself and God our Father, who loved us and through grace gave us eternal comfort and good hope, comfort your hearts and strengthen them in every good work and word.

2 THESSALONIANS 2:16-17 NRSV

God doesn't leave us alone in our weakness. When we feel incapable, he gives us the strength we lack to accomplish the task. When we are working sincerely for him, our work—no matter how insignificant it may seem—will always be effective.

We may feel like a failure in the eyes of those around us, but in the eyes of the Lord, our work done for his kingdom is never wasted. He cares enough about our hearts to comfort us in times of failure, and to value us in our moments of insignificance.

Lord, sometimes I feel that I have disappointed you. Despite my weakness, you comfort my heart and strengthen my soul. I know that in your eyes, I am never a failure. I am forever your beloved child.

Filling the Emptiness

O God, you are my God; earnestly I seek you;
my soul thirsts for you;
my flesh faints for you,
as in a dry and weary land where there is no water.

PSALM 63:1 ESV

We all experience seasons where we feel emptiness: an ache deep within us that is inexplicable but present all at once. In those times, when we aren't sure what it is that we're longing for, it is more of God that we need.

Deep in the heart of every person, there is an innate need for intimacy with our Creator. Without it our souls faint for want of him. But the beautiful truth is that he longs to fill us with himself. We have only to seek him in expectation.

Lord, I long for your presence. I need you desperately.
I pray that you would meet me in my emptiness
and fill me with your Spirit.

You Make Him Happy

The LORD will not forsake his people, for his great name's sake,
because it has pleased the LORD to make you a people for himself.

1 SAMUEL 12:22 ESV

What could be more rewarding than to know that you please the Lord?
When you enter into a relationship with God, he promises to never leave
you. He's with you for the long haul, not only because it's not in his nature
to leave, but also because—simply put—you make him happy.

Often we convince ourselves that we have disappointed God. This
translates into shame in our relationship with him. But God is pleased with
us, and he longs to speak that over us. Spend time today delighting yourself
in the Lord, and feeling his delight over you in return.

What a beautiful thing to know that I bring you pleasure, God.
Thank you for making me one of your people and for promising
to never leave me.

DAY 278

Stronger for Waiting

They who wait for the LORD shall renew their strength.
ISAIAH 40:31 ESV

Have you ever waited on someone? When you wait, you abdicate your ability to determine when something will happen. You are dependent on someone else.

When we wait on God, it can be incredibly difficult. Truly waiting on him means we aren't solving situations on our own. We wholly place our dependence and trust in God's solution, knowing it will be better than ours or anyone else's. Waiting is not natural. We would much prefer to act, even at the risk of acting incorrectly, than to wait on God. Even if we've waited a week or twenty years, his promise to us remains: if we persevere in waiting, we will become stronger.

Father, give me the fortitude to remain steadfast
in my waiting. Thank you for your promise that
I will be stronger if I wait.

Collected Tears

You have seen me tossing and turning through the night.
You have collected all my tears and preserved them in your bottle!
You have recorded every one in your book.

PSALM 56:8 TLB

Our grief is near to God's heart. He longs to console us: to stroke our hair, wipe our tears, and whisper comfort. He counts the nights we toss and turn; he collects our tears. God isn't absent in our sorrow, rather the opposite—he is closer than ever.

Don't be afraid to come to God with your grief. Share with him the deepest feelings in your heart without holding back. In his presence you will find comfort, hope, compassion, and more love than you could imagine.

Thank you, Jesus, for holding me in my sadness. I need your strength even more in my grief. Please be near to me and comfort me in your presence.

Learn from Me

*"Come to me, all you who are weary and burdened,
and I will give you rest."*
MATTHEW 11:28 NIV

Perhaps it's morning when you are reading this. Your day is just beginning, yet your heart is already heavy. Or maybe it's the end of the day and you feel weakened by the burdens you have taken on. Rest in the kindest person there ever was. Let his words soothe and strengthen you.

Perhaps you have taken on more than what God is asking you to—physically or emotionally. Christ himself makes it clear that his yoke is easy and his burden is light. If your yoke is too heavy, perhaps you aren't supposed to be carrying it in the first place. Learn from Jesus. Refusing wrong yokes won't necessarily feel natural to you. But ask and learn. As you do, he will strengthen your ability to know the difference, so you might enjoy his rest.

Jesus, help me learn from you and rest in you. I don't want to carry any yokes that you aren't asking me to. Give me wisdom and discernment as I walk into each new day.

Ask, Seek, Knock

"Ask and it will be given to you; seek and you will find; knock and the door will be opened to you. For everyone who asks receives; the one who seeks finds; and to the one who knocks, the door will be opened."

MATTHEW 7:7-8 NIV

Has your faith gotten weaker over time? Have some of your harder experiences left you more faithless than hopeful? Remember, regardless of the degree of your hard experiences, he promises to work everything out for good in your heart and life. Don't let your disappointments cloud the truth of God's Word. He promises that everyone who asks in his name receives.

Are you asking? Then you can count on receiving. Are you seeking? He promises you will find. Are you knocking? Yes, child, the door will be opened to you.

Father, please refresh me by the truth of your Word.
Help me to believe you again and with faith ask,
seek, and knock.

Committed to the Process

Put on your new nature, and be renewed as you learn
to know your Creator and become like him.

COLOSSIANS 3:10 NLT

While our salvation is a completed work, there is a continual working out of
our faith. This is because God has called you into a relationship with himself.
Relationships need to be nurtured and maintained. The word the Bible uses
for this concept is *renewal*.

Even after salvation, our new self is still being renewed in knowledge in
our Creator's image. Our minds also need continual renewal. Don't be
discouraged if you are still struggling with old ways of thinking or acting.
Renewal is a process. Continue to repent and submit yourself to God. He is
more passionate about renewing you than you are. He's a loving God who is
committed to the process.

*God, I'm sorry for all the times I fall short.
Help me to continually seek to renew my heart and my mind.
Show me how to become more like you.*

Freed for Life

"Let any one of you who is without sin be
the first to throw a stone at her."

JOHN 8:7 NIV

If you feel Jesus is holding back his love and compassion from you because
of something you have done or not done, think again! When Jesus died on
the cross, he mercifully forgave you.

Forgiveness is only appropriate when someone has done something wrong,
so God isn't hung up on your sin. Instead, God hung your sin on a cross and
set you unequivocally free! Enjoy living.

*Jesus, you didn't condemn the woman caught in adultery, and you
don't condemn me even though I deserve it. Thank you. Help me to
leave my sin behind and be fully cleansed by your work on the cross.*

Greater Works

"Most assuredly, I say to you, he who believes in Me,
the works that I do he will do also; and greater works
than these he will do, because I go to My Father."

JOHN 14:12 NKJV

The clock ticks and time passes as you wonder if you've made the most of each second. You seek meaning in the mundane, and you begin to wonder if you'll ever taste the miracle in the moment. You believe that God is capable of the impossible, but would he really use you to accomplish it? Is he great enough and powerful enough to transcend your mediocrity and turn the work of your hands into something that will last for eternity?

No matter what you believe you are capable of, God knows your intended purpose. Give yourself completely to him and he will accomplish things you could never have imagined. God can do great things through a surrendered life. All you have to do is the *surrender* part. He will do the rest.

*Heavenly Father, I surrender my life to you.
I want to be someone you can use to do great works
to the glory of your name. Have your way in my life.*

Always There for Me

God's way is perfect.
All the LORD's promises prove true.
He is a shield for all who look to him for protection.
For who is God except the LORD?
Who but our God is a solid rock?
PSALM 18:30-31 NLT

From famous songs to television commercials to close friends, there's a promise that is often made and rarely kept. *I'm here for you; you can always count on me.* Most of us have promised or have been promised this sometime in our life, and most have felt the sting of rejection or disappointment when things didn't turn out that way.

We say "nobody's perfect," but somehow we expect that everyone should be. In the midst of our trying circumstances, we call out to the people who promised to always be there, but they don't answer. They don't even call us back. Loved ones will hurt us because they are human. Even the best friend, the closest sister, the doting parent will fail in their ability to be there. There's no escaping it. But there is someone who you can always count on. You can tell him everything. He listens.

Father, help me to extend grace to those who have disappointed and hurt me. Thank you for being trustworthy and dependable. You truly are always there for me.

Never-changing Truth

Send out your light and your truth;
let them lead me;
let them bring me to your holy hill
and to your dwelling.

PSALM 43:3 NRSV

When we are weak, the enemy may just try to sneak in and pepper us with lies—to kick us while we're down. It's an incredibly effective tactic. Our best line of defense is to surround ourselves with the truth. Read it. Think it. Pray it. Declare it. In John 1:1, we read that the Word was with God in the beginning, and the Word was God. In Psalm 119:160, it says, "The very essence of your words is truth." Using simple logic, we put these Scriptures together and derive the following: If the Word is God and the Word is truth, then God is truth.

When you find yourself believing the lies of the enemy, turn to God's Word. Find your encouragement, joy, peace, and strength in his never-changing truth. No matter how many lies you have believed in the past, or how many you are believing right now, you can shut that deceptive voice down by saturating yourself in the truth of God's Word.

God, I expose the lies that I have believed about myself and others to your truth today. Help me to carefully consider what I hear and measure it against your truth. I choose not to believe anything that doesn't line up with your Word.

Knowing the Shepherd

"My sheep hear my voice, and I know them, and they follow me.
I give them eternal life, and they will never perish,
and no one will snatch them out of my hand."

JOHN 10:27-28 ESV

An international festival is held each year and the most popular event showcases the talents of Irish sheep dogs. The shepherd uses whistles and quiet voice commands to direct the dog, who in turn herds the sheep through various obstacles and dangers. Audiences marvel at the speed of the dogs and the swift changes in the herd's direction, all due to the effective communication between man, dog, and sheep.

Jesus often spoke about shepherds, calling himself our Good Shepherd. His followers understood that sheep need help through many obstacles and dangers, just as we do. And we need Jesus to communicate with us in a quiet, familiar voice so we will know which way to turn for safety. Our shepherd has one goal: keep his lambs safe. He hems us in with gentle calls and prodding where necessary. He understands our limits, our tendency to wander, our nature to rebel. In his goodness, he nudges our sides, reminding us to trust him and obey his commands.

*Jesus, thank you for your voice that leads me.
I want to hear from you today. I sit quietly and wait for you,
knowing you always have the right thing to say.*

A Life of Victory

Can anything ever separate us from Christ's love? Does it mean he no longer
loves us if we have trouble or calamity, or are persecuted, or hungry, or
destitute, or in danger, or threatened with death? No, despite all these
things, overwhelming victory is ours through Christ, who loved us.

ROMANS 8:35, 37 NLT

The Miracle Mop promised to be the solution for every mopping mess.
No more stubborn stains, stuck-on grime, or back-breaking scrubbing and
scouring. The solution was simple and cheap! Such assurances tug at our
pocketbooks because… well… life is messy and sometimes a short-cut is
downright tantalizing! But we know it's never that easy. The mop doesn't
push itself, after all!

It's tempting to take short-cuts, but a life of victory isn't a life without
disappointment or hard work. Jesus promised us trials and difficulties as
we follow him. Jesus' promise was meant to prepare us for the rejection,
bitterness, and hatred we would encounter. Jesus also promised us grace,
strength, hope, and victory. Don't be deceived to think that good works,
prayers, or even faith will produce a life of ease and earthly blessing,
showered down from above. We have one promise of victory and that is
the saving love of Jesus Christ.

God, your love is victorious in all situations. I say today that I am
willing to scrub and scour. I don't want to take shortcuts. Give me
eyes to see the things that matter and the strength to go after them.

Broken Fragments

He will take our weak mortal bodies and change them into
glorious bodies like his own, using the same power with which
he will bring everything under his control.

PHILIPPIANS 3:21 NLT

When a flower pot crashes to the pavement or a vase shatters to the
floor, we consider the damage in hopes that it can be repaired. What is
left? Dangerously tiny shards of glass, too small to piece back together? Or
simple, bulky pieces, like those of a puzzle, needing only glue and patience?
One thing is certain: we will work harder to fix something that has great
value to us.

Just like the broken pottery, we are broken vessels in need of extensive
repairs. No elaborate doctoring is required, however, just the humblest
of procedures. We hold out our hands and give our broken, desperate,
painful, sinful, prideful selves over to the one who mends us into wholeness
without a single remaining scar or crack.

*God, I marvel at your ability to piece even the tiniest fragments of
my broken life back together. You are both holy and whole, and I am
your creation. I submit to you, knowing that your healing work never
leaves a scar and your abiding love makes me whole forever.*

Asking for Wisdom

Listen carefully to wisdom;
set your mind on understanding.
Cry out for wisdom,
and beg for understanding.

PROVERBS 2:2-3 NCV

Grief has a funny way of messing with our heads. It can cause a fog to roll in and settle over our minds. Small decisions feel like monstrous ones, or maybe it's the opposite: big decisions are made hastily because, quite frankly, we don't have the energy to think everything through. So how do we get the wisdom we need for the task set before us? We ask God for it.

King Solomon was put in charge of a nation. He knew it was an impossible task to complete without wisdom. He wasn't born the wisest man who ever lived; he acquired his wisdom by asking God to give it to him. If God can give Solomon wisdom to run a kingdom, he can certainly give us wisdom to make decisions about big and small things in our lives.

God, I need wisdom every day. Thank you that you want me to ask you for it. Help me to hear it in whatever form it comes—directly from you or through the sound advice of family, friends, or counselors.

Getting Back

As for you, return to your God,
hold fast to love and justice,
and wait continually for your God.

HOSEA 12:6 NRSV

Sometimes we lose our way and lose sight of the passion we once felt for God. Once we've lost our connection with him, we don't always know how to get back. We wonder if there is too much between us that he can't overlook.

But it's as simple as returning; as straightforward as getting down on your knees and saying, "God, I'm back." When you return, holding fast to the love that first drew you to him, God will show himself to you.

God, I know that there are areas of my life where I've put distance between myself and you. I don't want to continue with a disconnect between us. I want to return to you and be restored to right relationship. Thank you that even when I wandered, you never went anywhere.

The Secrets of God

"Can you understand the secrets of God?
Can you search the limits of the Almighty?"

JOB 11:7 NCV

Have you ever discovered something about yourself that you never knew before? Maybe you tried a new food that you always claimed you hated, and you found you actually loved it. Maybe you were surprised by an idea you had that you didn't even know you were capable of.

If we, who are human, are so complex that we don't fully know ourselves, then how much more complex is the God who created us? We mustn't limit God to what we think we know of him. We cannot know his limits. But we can trust in his Word and his Holy Spirit to teach us as we seek to know him more.

Almighty God, help me not to limit you to what I've seen or what I've heard of you. Help me to constantly be seeking your heart so that I can know you for myself.

Fill Our Hunger

"I am the bread of life. Whoever comes to me will
never be hungry, and whoever believes in me will
never be thirsty."

JOHN 6:35 NRSV

You don't have to teach babies to put things in their mouth—they are born
with a natural instinct to feed themselves. But you do need to teach them
what to feed themselves.

We were all created with a natural spiritual hunger for God. But we must
learn how to fill our hunger. There are things that we will try to put into our
souls that will never satisfy us. The only true remedy to the deepest longing
in our being is God—because we were created to hunger after him.

*Lord, help me not to look to outside sources to fill the hunger that can
only be satisfied by relationship with you. Help me to recognize my
hunger so that instead of living as one who is empty, I can live as one
who is full of your presence.*

I Am Accepted

If you confess with your mouth that Jesus is Lord and believe in
your heart that God raised him from the dead, you will be saved.
For with the heart one believes and is justified, and with the mouth
one confesses and is saved.
ROMANS 10:9-10 ESV

How can it be that a humble prayer, a simple and yet astounding desire
to lay down one's life and take up a life like Jesus Christ, establishes our
eternity in the kingdom of heaven? We live in a world where, more often
than not, we get what we deserve and nothing comes easy.

Sometimes, because we can't believe that acceptance can come from such
a simple act, we reconstruct the gospel. We want to feel like we deserve
God's grace, or that we have earned it, or that we've traded fairly. We build
another set of requirements: more praying, more giving, more reading,
more serving. Quiet time. Worship team. Children's ministry. Bible study.
All of these habits are good and Christ-like, but they don't guarantee *more*
acceptance. Not from God, anyway.

God, thank you that the path to salvation really is simple. I don't
have to earn it. I believe it. I confess it. My simple and earnest prayer
assures me of acceptance into your family.

Good Plans

For I know the plans I have for you, declares the LORD,
plans for welfare and not for evil,
to give you a future and a hope.

JEREMIAH 29:11 ESV

There are two types of people in the world: those who can pack their bags at a moment's notice and take a last-minute vacation to Paris, and those who need months of planning and organization. You may be willing to do either one—it is a trip to Paris, after all!—but under which conditions would you most enjoy yourself? Could you trust that it would be everything you would've planned for yourself if you didn't thoroughly prepare it?

When we consider our future, it can be difficult to trust that things will work out the way we desire. If only we could know that the plans for our future are certain! Consider that God knows the future, he knows you, and he knows exactly what you need.

God, I choose to believe that you have the best plan in mind for my life. You can show me the secret places and hidden gems that I would never find on my own.

Child of God

All who are led by the Spirit of God are children of God.
ROMANS 8:14 NLT

God is a good Father! He loves you with a love that is matchless and unwavering. Our earthly fathers have important jobs; primarily, they guide us to the love of our heavenly Father. Whether a devoted man's guidance models the Father's truly perfect and boundless love, or a flawed man's brokenness leads us to the Father's healing and compassionate love, both lead us home as children of God.

With lives submitted to Jesus Christ, we have the privilege of the Holy Spirit leading us in truth and in action. This Spirit, as Paul describes, is proof that we are adopted into God's family. By faith, we can take hold of our claim as God's precious and beloved children.

Thank you, heavenly Father, for your loving authority, gentle guidance, unending grace, tender compassion, fierce protection, and perfect faithfulness. I am so blessed to have your inheritance of life everlasting.

Perseverance

Do not throw away this confident trust in the Lord.
Remember the great reward it brings you! Patient endurance
is what you need now, so that you will continue to do God's will.
Then you will receive all that he has promised.

HEBREWS 10:35-36 NLT

Do you remember when you first decided to follow Christ? Maybe you felt
like a huge weight was being lifted off you, or that the peace and joy you'd
been searching for was finally yours. You were filled with excitement in
your newfound life, and you felt ready to take on the world in the name
of Jesus.

Following God may come easy at first. We accept him into our lives and
are swept into his love with incredible hope. But as time goes on, old
temptations return, and threaten to shake our resolve. The confidence
we felt in our relationship at first lessens as we wonder if we have what
it takes to stick it out in this Christian life. Remain confident in him;
he will accomplish what he has promised. When following him gets hard,
press in even harder and remember that you will be richly rewarded for
your perseverance.

*God, help me to remain in a place of complete confidence
and trust in you. I want to step boldly into all that you have for me.*

Walk Steady

Direct my footsteps according to your word;
let no sin rule over me.

PSALM 119:133 NIV

What is it about high heels? Every family album contains a photo of an
adorable toddler attempting to walk in those shoes, and every woman
remembers her wobbly attempt to appear graceful in that first pair of
pumps. Most of us also have a memory of a not-so-graceful stumble
or even a twisted ankle; yet, somehow the stiletto retains its appeal.
Who hasn't relied on the steady arm of an escort or companion in far more
sensible footwear?

Walking with Jesus is a little like learning to walk in four-inch heels. Others
make it look so easy, gliding along apparently sinless while we feel shaky
and uncertain, prone to stumble at any moment. Will we take a wrong step?
Fall flat on our faces? (Do anyone else's feet hurt?) Lean on the strong arm
of the Savior; allow him to steady you and direct your steps.

*Lord, I know I am not confident in all areas of my
walk with you. I ask for your guidance and steady hand.
Lead me in all that I venture out to do. I trust you.*

Made to Be

The fruit of the Spirit is love, joy, peace, patience, kindness, goodness, faithfulness, gentleness, self-control; against such things there is no law.
GALATIANS 5:22-23 ESV

Making applesauce with autumn's abundant apple harvest is a beloved pastime across northern parts of America. Experts have developed award-winning recipes whose secret, they say, is combining multiple varieties of apples to produce a complex flavor profile. The result is a balance of the tart, sweet, crisp, mellow, and bold flavors for which apples are so well-loved. Each variety of apple is essential to the applesauce; their distinct flavors mesh into a delicious thing of beauty.

In the applesauce of God's ministry, each believer's spiritual fruit flavor-profile is essential. When we compare the evidence of our fruit against other believers, lies are whispered to our flesh: *your fruit isn't as shiny, your fruit isn't as fragrant, your fruit is too mushy and flavorless.* All trees shouldn't produce the same fruit.

Lord, help me to be grateful for the fruit that I bear. Help me not to compare my fruit with those around me. Thank you for creating me with a distinct flavor and uniqueness.

The Wisdom Request

If any of you lacks wisdom, you should ask God,
who gives generously to all without finding fault,
and it will be given to you.

JAMES 1:5 NIV

In the first chapter of James, the apostle encourages the believers to welcome troubles because the testing of their faith will grow endurance. And when their endurance reaches maturity, they will be entirely complete in Christ, needing nothing. James exhorts them to ask for wisdom during the difficulty and God will give it generously.

During periods of trial, our need for divine wisdom is great—not only to know how to navigate the details, but for comfort, mental clarity, and the ability to make wise choices. Our cry to God should not be necessarily for the removal of hardship, but for wisdom to make the right use of it. Are you in need of wisdom from God at this moment? Ask him. He wants you to. He has promised to give it unsparingly.

Lord, today I need a large dose of divine wisdom.
I'm unsure as to how to manage my hardship as well as my own spirit.
Thank you that you will guide me through this day one step at a time.

Thirst

"Come, all you who are thirsty,
come to the waters;
and you who have no money,
come, buy and eat!
Come, buy wine and milk
without money and without cost."

ISAIAH 55:1 NIV

Thirst is a God-given sensation to let us know we need a drink. Under normal circumstances, the solution for a thirst problem is really simple. Just take a drink. Spiritual thirst is also God-given. He created us to be satisfied at only one fountain: Jesus himself—the living water. Without him we are barren and dry. Jesus told the woman at the well that if she drank the water he gave to her, she would never thirst again. He spoke of himself.

Isaiah 55:1 reveals the way to satisfy a spiritual thirst. Just come to Jesus. Money isn't needed; the only cost is surrender. Drink of the wine of the Holy Spirit and the milk of the Word, and you will be satisfied. Are you feeling spiritually dry today? Have you been too busy to eat and drink properly to satisfy your soul?

Jesus, forgive me for neglecting to drink from the fountain of your Word. I need a fresh drink of living water. Fill me up today, Lord; quench my thirst.

Valuable

"What is the price of five sparrows—two copper coins? Yet God does
not forget a single one of them. And the very hairs on your head are all
numbered. So don't be afraid; you are more valuable to God than
a whole flock of sparrows."

LUKE 12:6-7 NLT

Jesus loved to use simple stories and illustrations to teach spiritual truths.
Here he is explaining the value of human life by using sparrows as an
example. While Matthew tells us that two birds could be acquired for one
cent, Luke reveals the five-for-the-price-of-four deal. Sparrows were of so
little value that if you purchased four, the fifth one was thrown in for free.
Nearly worthless creatures, yet unforgotten by the Father.

Are you feeling forgotten today? Is fear crouching at your door because
of it? Remember this: God cares about every little detail of your life to
the extent of counting and numbering the hairs on your head. You are his
precious, valuable creation. It was an understatement when he said, "You
are worth more to me than a whole flock of sparrows." Can you receive
that today? Will you?

*Oh, Lord, thank you for being such a loving Creator and Father. You
care about every detail of my life. I don't need to be afraid because
you are watching over me with tender loving care.*

What God Wants

The Lord has told you, human, what is good;
he has told you what he wants from you:
to do what is right to other people,
love being kind to others,
and live humbly, obeying your God.

MICAH 6:8 NCV

Have you ever wondered how you can ever make up for your failings? Should you try harder, give more, do more things for God? Maybe you have a vague sense that you just don't measure up when it comes to being an effective servant of Christ. In Micah's day, Israel wondered what would satisfy the justice of God: sacrifice one animal, or a thousand, or even their own children to compensate for their sin? God did not need their sacrifices and religious exercises. He simply wanted Israel to live in humble obedience to him, and to do what was right.

And that's the message for you today. Don't make your Christian life too complicated. Don't worry about doing more. Walk simply and humbly before your God: obey him, be kind to others, and do what is right.

Thank you, Lord, for giving me clear directives in your Word. Even though they are simple, they are not easy. I need your help today to live humbly before you and to do what is right.

When You Have Jesus

By his divine power, God has given us everything we need for living a godly life. We have received all of this by coming to know him, the one who called us to himself by means of his marvelous glory and excellence.

2 PETER 1:3 NLT

A young mom had a handicapped child and a severely ill husband both in the hospital at the same time. Her faith in God was evident as she greeted people with a cheerful countenance. "How do you do it?" she was asked. With a smile she answered, "I have Jesus."

Is Jesus enough for you? Think for a minute about all the wonderful things you have in Christ: his amazing promises, eternal life, forgiveness, power, help, strength, peace, guidance—everything you need for living a godly life. The problem for many is that they don't appropriate God's truth into their daily lives. They read it, but it lies dormant and unattended. Is that you today?

Lord, thank you for calling me to yourself and giving me everything I need to live for you. Help me to know you better and take hold of your magnificent promises. I want to experience your all-sufficiency.

DAY 305

A Song of Delight

The LORD your God is living among you.
He is a mighty savior.
He will take delight in you with gladness.
With his love, he will calm all your fears.
He will rejoice over you with joyful songs.

ZEPHANIAH 3:17 NLT

Wouldn't you say that a grandma's feelings about her grandchildren can be summarized in the word "delight?" Listen to the synonyms: adore, cherish, relish, and revel in. Grandma plays silly games, buys toys, and showers her grandkids with love. Now, transfer this very human experience to the perfect, supernatural divine experience. God, our Savior who lives in and among us, delights in us with more intensity than any number of synonyms could capture. His love is so strong, our fears are calmed. His delight bursts forth from divine lips in joyful songs over us! It's no wonder there is in the heart of man a desire to worship—to sing back to God with similar delight!

Take a moment today and revel in the fact that God delights in you. He knows your weaknesses and flaws, but still rejoices over you. In demonstrating such amazing love, he calms all of your fears. Sing a song of praise back to him!

Lord, it's amazing to realize that you really do delight in me far more than I can comprehend. Thank you for your incredible love.
I praise and worship you today.

Recorded Wrongs

[Love] keeps no record of wrongs.
1 CORINTHIANS 13:5 NIV

Many experts agree that one of the ways to keep relationships healthy and strong is to avoid phrases like "you always…", "you never…", or "I can't believe you did this again!" True love releases past mistakes and genuinely believes for the best next time. This gives freedom from guilt, and permission for the relationship to move on and grow.

This truth applies to everyone we interact with in life. Let's not keep track of people by their offenses and label them for their mistakes. Let's give freedom to grow and learn. God keeps no record of confessed wrongs. Release yourself from regrets, and live in God's freedom.

Lord, I confess that I have held resentment in my heart toward people who have offended me. I release those wrongs to you now and ask you to help me erase them from my heart. You are perfect in your love for me, and I want to be more like you.

Generosity of Time

Each of you should give what you have decided in your heart to give,
not reluctantly or under compulsion, for God loves a cheerful giver.

2 CORINTHIANS 9:7 NIV

Sometimes it is easier to be generous with our money than our time. Life is usually so busy that we tend to guard our time religiously. Often we get so focused on ourselves and our own to-do list that we fail to notice the needs around us. Perhaps a friend could use a phone call, or an elderly neighbor help with planting her garden. Maybe volunteer hours could be a blessing to a teacher, or someone at church who needs help moving.

We are called to be the hands and feet of Christ. There are so many opportunities to serve others around us, and there are such blessings to be found when we do. Sometimes giving of yourself is more valuable than a hastily written check. God loves a cheerful giver. Be that cheerful giver, even if it means laying aside your own needs or schedule. Think about how you could bless someone with your time.

God, show me how I can bless someone
with my time today. I want to give cheerfully
even if it means I have to lay aside my own needs.

Application Accepted

Long ago, even before he made the world, God chose us to be his very own through what Christ would do for us; he decided then to make us holy in his eyes, without a single fault—we who stand before him covered with his love.

EPHESIANS 1:4 TLB

Applications are essential for gleaning the promising applicants from the inadequate. Fill out this form, and find out if you're approved for a home loan, for college admittance, for a credit card. We put our best qualities on paper, tweak our weaknesses, and hope for approval. But rejection is always a possibility.

With God, however, our acceptance has already been promised. We must only appeal to his Son, Jesus, who steps in on our behalf and petitions for our approval. There is no credit flaw, no failing grade, and no past default that his death on the cross doesn't redeem completely. Because we are covered with his loving forgiveness, there is no flaw in us. We are accepted by God as part of his family and redeemed by his grace for his eternal kingdom.

God, I stand on the promise that there is nothing in my history—
no past or present sin—that can separate me from your love.
I cast everything on you and believe I am wholly accepted
and abundantly loved!

A Warm Welcome

Accept one another, then, just as Christ accepted you,
in order to bring praise to God.
ROMANS 15:7 NIV

Have you ever met someone and immediately felt a connection? Maybe you were drawn to their personality and a friendship was born. Have you ever met someone you struggled to connect with? Maybe the way they dressed, acted, talked, or chose their career was completely foreign to you.

We all have our natural friendships. We don't have to be best friends with everyone we meet because the truth of it is, we won't. But what if, despite our differences, we still accepted all those we come in contact with? As Christians, our main goal is to bring praise to God. By accepting others with the same measure of absolute acceptance that Christ extends to us, we honor God and bring him praise.

God, help me today to accept those around me,
and to genuinely welcome them with open arms
in spite of our differences.

The Father's Love

> "If a man has a hundred sheep but one of the sheep gets lost, he will leave the other ninety-nine on the hill and go to look for the lost sheep. I tell you the truth, if he finds it he is happier about that one sheep than about the ninety-nine that were never lost."
>
> MATTHEW 18:12-13 NCV

Regardless of how beautifully or imperfectly your earthly father showed his love, your heavenly Father's love is utterly boundless. Rest in that thought a moment. There is nothing you can do to change how he feels about you. Nothing.

We spend so much time trying to make ourselves more lovable, from beauty regimens to gourmet baking, to being there for pretty much everyone. It's easy to forget we are already perfectly loved. Our Father loves us more than we can imagine. And he would do anything for us. Anything.

God I thank you that the love I have for my very closest companion is a mere fraction of the love you have for me. I am amazed by your immeasurable, great love for me.

Deeper Roots

"The one on whom seed was sown on the good soil, this is the man who hears the word and understands it; who indeed bears fruit and brings forth, some a hundredfold, some sixty, and some thirty."

MATTHEW 13:23 NASB

Calla lilies are beautiful flowers with wide, spotted leaves, thick stems, and bold colors. Year after year, you can watch the stunning leaves appear, and anticipate the gorgeous flowers… and then be disappointed when nothing more happens. Perhaps the soil is the problem? Calla lilies can be very particular.

It's a great picture of Jesus' parable of the sower and the seeds. Some seeds fall on rocky soil, and while God's Word is received, it doesn't take firm root and quickly withers at the sign of hardship. The seeds that are established in good soil, where the roots can go deep, not only survive, they also bear fruit.

God, I long to see more depth in my relationship with you.
I want others to see your beauty displayed in my life.
Help me to plant myself in fertile soil so I can hear,
understand, and bear fruit for your glory.

Better than Rubies

Receive my instruction, and not silver,
And knowledge rather than choice gold;
For wisdom is better than rubies,
And all the things one may desire
cannot be compared with her.

PROVERBS 8:10-11 NKJV

If you were granted the one thing that you desire most, what would it be? We can probably answer this question better if we think of who or what we idolize. Whose life do we want, or what quality do we most admire? Beauty, intelligence, creativity, recognition, or love?

King Solomon understood the value of wisdom better than any other. When God offered him anything he desired, King Solomon responded with a request for wisdom. He could have asked for fame, or riches, or success in warfare; instead, he asked for *understanding*. King Solomon sought knowledge and instruction first, and ended up being the most wise, wealthy, famous, successful king that ever lived.

God, I recognize the value of wisdom today. Give me deeper understanding of your Word and the world around me. Help me to seek after your wisdom as I would seek for gold, silver, and jewels.

Adornment

*Do not let your adornment be merely outward—arranging the hair,
wearing gold, or putting on fine apparel— rather let it be
the hidden person of the heart, with the incorruptible beauty of a
gentle and quiet spirit, which is very precious in the sight of God.*

1 PETER 3:3-4 NKJV

Women like to look their best. This usually means wearing the right
clothes, hairstyle, and accessories to match. Sometimes just getting our
hair right can be the difference between a good or bad day! We need to
admitour superficial nature and recognize when we are prioritizing outward
appearance over inner beauty.

The Bible doesn't condemn outward adornment; rather, it is advises that
we pay more attention to the "hidden person of the heart." Who is on the
inside? Are you doing your best to make that person beautiful? Beauty,
to God, is a gentle and quiet spirit.

*Lord, I know I don't always act in gentleness toward others. I know
I could do better maintaining a quiet spirit. Help me develop and
display these qualities that are truly beautiful.*

A Strong, Graceful Oak

To all who mourn… he will give: beauty for ashes;
joy instead of mourning;
praise instead of heaviness.
For God has planted them like strong
and graceful oaks for his own glory.

ISAIAH 61:3 TLB

How many thoughts does the human brain conceive in an hour? In a day? In a lifetime? How many of those thoughts are about God: who he is and what he has done for his children? Imagine your own thoughts about life—grocery lists, dentist appointments, song lyrics, lost keys—and your thoughts about God—his majesty, holiness, comfort, creativity—weighed against each other on a scale. Likely, it would tip in favor of the many details of human existence.

These temporary details overshadow the one comfort and promise we can rely on: the gospel of Jesus' birth, death, resurrection, and ascension for our eternal salvation. Wipe every other thought away and we are left with this truth. For those burdened by their sin it is of great comfort! Jesus came to give us new life!

God, thank you that I am not a weak sapling, limited by inadequate light and meager nourishment. You have made me a strong and graceful oak, soaring and resilient for your glory.

Strength of His Presence

Seek the LORD and his strength;
seek his presence continually!

1 CHRONICLES 16:11 ESV

Our lives demand strength. There are many situations that we find ourselves in that test what we're made of. We do our best to be strong and to meet each challenge head on, but we consistently come up short. What we often fail to recognize is that it's only in our weakness that the perfect strength of God can be shown.

We have a God who fights for us. A God who bends down his ear to our cry and who lends his strength for the battle. When we seek to dwell in the place of his presence daily, we will find his strength in our hearts and his power in our spirits.

Lord, I am weak. There are things in my life that have beaten me down and have only served to amplify my need for you. I am here today asking for your strength and for your presence. I need you in every part of my life.

The Lord Is Near

The LORD is near to all who call on him,
to all who call on him in truth.
He fulfills the desire of those who fear him;
he also hears their cry and saves them.

PSALM 145:18-19 ESV

The Lord is not only near to those who call on him every single morning. He's not only near to those who live a sinless life or those who speak with eloquence. God is near to all who call on him in truth. He is near to everyone whose heart is genuine before him. God's love is enough to close the distance between heaven and earth and to allow our voice to be heard.

Do you long for the presence of God? Then step into it. It is truly that simple. There are days when we miss his presence and we desire his closeness, but we forget in that moment that it's always been ours for the taking. Jesus demolished every single barrier that ever stood between you and God. Quiet your heart, enter his presence, and speak your mind. He listens, he cares, and he answers.

Heavenly Father, thank you that you are near to me.
Thank you that I don't have to jump through hoops to stand
in your presence. You are a good Father, a loving God.
Hear my heart today and give me the peace to wait for your answer.

The Whisper

This is what the high and exalted One says—
he who lives forever, whose name is holy:
"I live in a high and holy place,
but also with the one who is contrite and lowly in spirit,
to revive the spirit of the lowly
and to revive the heart of the contrite."

ISAIAH 57:15 NIV

What is it about the night that turns our thoughts on him? We collapse into bed, exhausted from the day, and in the darkness we whisper out to him: "I need you. I've missed your presence." And the tears fall, and repentance comes, and the heart opens, and the Spirit moves. And you realize all at once in the darkness that he is just a whisper away. He's never been far, never as far as you felt.

His presence brings immediate healing and his closeness restores our souls. In human relationship, when there is distance between two people it damages the relationship and it makes it difficult to move forward. But in our relationship with the Lord, no matter how much distance we create between ourselves and him, we can always be immediately, wholly restored. All it takes is a whisper in the dark, calling on his name—the name that heals us, restores us, and starts us all over again.

Jesus, I need you. Erase the distance between us
and restore me fully in your presence.

True Peace

"I leave you peace; my peace I give you. I do not give
it to you as the world does. So don't let your hearts
be troubled or afraid."

JOHN 14:27 NCV

What is peace? A moment of true relaxation? An hour of quiet calm? Ease of life and circumstance? Our definitions of peace may make us feel peaceful, but do they line up with the true definition given by the peace giver himself?

Jesus says very plainly that his peace isn't the same as the world's peace. He does not give it in the same way that the world gives—a way that comes and goes and can be claimed or lost at any instant. His peace is not dependent on mood or circumstance, position or company. His peace is inward. It's a lack of fear. It's the absence of anxiety. It's the knowledge that no matter what loudness, what weariness, what complications surround you—you are held.

*Lord Jesus, I worry and fear about so many things.
I unknowingly exchange your peace for the world's peace that is
fleeting and unsure. But I crave your true peace, the peace that will
not come and go with each passing circumstance.*

Purpose to My Pain

The LORD will fulfill his purpose for me;
your steadfast love, O LORD, endures forever.
Do not forsake the work of your hands.

PSALM 138:8 ESV

Life often doesn't turn out the way we think it should. When we're stuck in the midst of circumstances we never wanted—dreams lost and hope buried—it's difficult to find meaning in it all, and it can seem impossible to keep going. But God gives purpose to our pain and hope to carry on.

When it feels a lot more like we're surviving in him rather than actively abiding in him, he comforts us with the promise that he will complete the work he began in us, making all things beautiful in his time. We have the blessing of embracing all that is going on in our lives as part of his trustworthy plan to glorify himself and to accomplish his loving intentions for us.

God, I believe you are molding me more into the image of Jesus through the painful circumstances in my life. I hope and trust in your promise that you will fulfill your purpose in me.

Broken Relationships

Draw near to God, and he will draw near to you. Cleanse your hands, you sinners, and purify your hearts, you double-minded. Do not speak evil against one another, brothers. The one who speaks against a brother or judges his brother, speaks evil against the law and judges the law.

JAMES 4:8, 11 ESV

We were created for relationship. Since Adam expressed the need for a companion, people have sought fellowship together. But no matter how strong our desire to have healthy, loving relationships, it can be hard to move past the pain of a broken one. It may be a divorce, an estranged sister or mother, or a longtime friend who has somehow become a bitter rival. In order for reconciliation to take place, we must look to God for direction.

First, pray. Submit yourself to God and refuse to allow the enemy any further destruction. Next, ask him what sin, if any, you have committed to contribute to the dissent. Confess it, repent, and let it go. Now comes the hard part: don't speak out against them. Don't slander or gossip or share your grievance; it won't make things better. In fact, it only makes things worse.

Father God, I extend forgiveness today instead of judgment. I am sorry for my part in this broken relationship. Help me to let your love flow through me and onto those with whom I am at odds. I humbly ask you for reconciliation and restoration.

Remember Your Wonders

I will remember the deeds of the LORD;
yes, I will remember your wonders of old.

PSALM 77:11 ESV

When we find ourselves doubting God's power to work miracles in our lives, we must remember the wonders he has performed throughout history. Scripture is full of accounts of lives changed by the power of God.

The same great God who raised Lazarus from the dead is the God we worship today. The God who gave sight to a blind man and who let a lame man get up and walk still works miracles. Believe God for something great, knowing that his power has never lessened and his wonders never cease.

God, I am amazed at the wonders you have performed throughout history. Help me to recall your power when I begin to doubt your strength. Thank you for redeeming me and allowing me, through faith, to witness your miracles in my own life. Help me to grow in faith and expectation of your greatness.

DAY 322

Because of the Poor

The LORD says,
"I will now rise up,
because the poor are being hurt.
Because of the moans of the helpless,
I will give them the help they want."

PSALM 12:5 NCV

God's economy is completely opposite from our own. Our currency is money and power, while his are mercy and grace. Our society elevates the rich and prominent, God lifts up the needy and nameless. His main objective isn't getting something from people; it's lavishing himself on them. His heart lies with the poor. He is a defender of the helpless and a protector of the weak.

If we desire to please the heart of the Father, then we too will take up the cause of the poor. We will defend them, rescue them, and help them. We will speak for them, honor them, and lavish love on them.

Father, I know that your heart is tender toward the needy.
Put opportunities in my path to meet the needs of the poor
and to serve the helpless.

Fully Devoted

"Don't urge me to leave you or to turn back from you.
Where you go I will go, and where you stay I will stay.
Your people will be my people and your God my God."

RUTH 1:16 NIV

Ruth gave up everything she'd ever known to follow Naomi back to Bethlehem—a land completely foreign to her. What a radical commitment: to leave everything familiar for the sake of devotion to another!

Are you willing to leave everything you love and know to follow God? He is a God who rewards and repays. Everything you give up for the kingdom will be restored to you in an even greater measure than you gave up.

Heavenly Father, I want to be willing to go
wherever you lead me—even if it takes me
to places I've never been. You are my God,
and I am fully devoted to you.

Human Empathy

Rejoice with those who rejoice,
weep with those who weep.

ROMANS 12:15 ESV

There are few things more remarkable than the power of human empathy. When someone is hurt, we can feel their pain although we are not wounded. When someone cries, we can weep with them although we are not sad. When someone laughs, we can enjoy the moment with them although the happiness is not our own.

Jesus came to us, as a human, in the greatest act of empathy in history. As we follow his example by shouldering each other's sorrows and by sharing in another's joy, we express his heart to the world.

Lord, give me a capacity for empathy that will minister your character to those around me. Help me to better understand what others are going through so that I can reveal your heart to those around me.

Make a Change

Do not conform to the pattern of this world, but be transformed
by the renewing of your mind. Then you will be able to test and approve
what God's will is—his good, pleasing and perfect will.
ROMANS 12:2 NIV

We want change, but we struggle to get or stay on task with our goals.
"One day, I'll…" is the enemy of "Today, I am…"; yet it seems that as long
as change hurts more than staying the same, we vacillate between our
desires and our comfort.

It is often so with surrendering to the Holy Spirit. He longs to do "greater
things than these," and while this appeals to us, the comfort of doing
nothing seems reassuring, safe, and predictable. We find, at last, that the
center of God's will truly is the safest place for our lives. Knowing that,
we revel in him as he molds and inspires us. We were created to do
good things.

*Thank you, Father, for the changes you are making
in my life. I enjoy being transformed by you,
polished like the silver brought out for
special occasions.*

Uniquely Cared For

Just as each of us has one body with many members, and these members do not all have the same function, so in Christ we, though many, form one body, and each member belongs to all the others.

ROMANS 12:4-5 NIV

Each of us has a function. We don't operate like one another because we aren't fashioned that way. We often don't agree upon priorities—beyond dwelling in Christ and living in love—because we are each made to carry different aspects of God's glory.

So often, we read this verse as an adjuration to play nicely with people of other denominations. That's not it, though. It's a glorification of our wondrously creative God, and an encouragement to each take up our gifts, allowing others to do the same. Our gifts are just as personal as our salvation experiences. When we finally embrace our interdependence, we honor each other and operate in unity. We embrace who we are in Christ and let go of what we are not. To have the liberty to do so is an aspect of what it is to be truly free in Christ, and to operate in freedom.

Father, thank you for the intricate care you used in making me. Help me to recognize what gifts within me are actually not universal values for everyone else, but are your unique signature of grace upon my life. I love you!

Leveling Up

Trust in the LORD with all your heart,
and do not lean on your own understanding.
In all your ways acknowledge him,
and he will make straight your paths.

PROVERBS 3:5-6 ESV

As we learn to walk in surrender to the Holy Spirit, our heavenly Father beckons us to a higher level of intimacy with him. In order to do this, we must become vulnerable and get real with him. We must continually trust him more than our experiences or reasoning.

When we trust God without boundaries, we find him more reliable than anyone else. We are wrapped in his love—the safest place we could find ourselves. Constantly leaning our hearts toward him, and choosing what he would, we receive his comfort and guidance, and our paths become straight.

*Heavenly Father, I come to you and ask you
to help me trust you, knowing that you have
the best in store for me. Have your way with me.
I release control, and I trust in you. You are for me,
not against me. I love you.*

The Irony of Weakness

The LORD is the everlasting God,
the Creator of all the earth.
He never grows weak or weary.
No one can measure the depths of his understanding.
He gives power to the weak
and strength to the powerless.

ISAIAH 40:28-29 NLT

When you are stripped of your talents and strengths, you can do nothing but rely on the grace of God to carry you further. It is there, in your lacking, that God's power is truly revealed. None of us likes to feel inadequate, but if our inadequacy can further reveal Christ in us, it is always worth it.

We must remember that we are vessels of mercy—hallowed images of his grace that exist to always, first and foremost, bring glory to Christ.

In my weakness, Lord, be my strength.
Reveal yourself through me so that I can join you
in accomplishing your work.

Sacrifice of Thanksgiving

Offer to God a sacrifice of thanksgiving
Call upon Me in the day of trouble;
I shall rescue you, and you will honor Me.

PSALM 50:14-15 NASB

The Israelites in the Old Testament had a complicated list of rituals and sacrifices to follow. Among the five special offerings, one was the peace offering, or the sacrifice of thanksgiving. When Jesus came, the old requirements were replaced by the new so that our worship could be an expression of our hearts directly through our lips.

It's not always easy to be thankful. In times of great difficulty when everything in the natural screams "I don't like this!" gratitude comes at great sacrifice. It is a denial of the natural response, dying to one's own preference, and in submission saying, "God, your way is best and I thank you." Having a grateful heart gives us the privilege of calling on God in our day of trouble and the assurance of his deliverance. Can you offer God your sacrifice of praise today?

Lord, today I want to say thanks for being my God
and for the grace you show me each day. As I call out
to you, I know you will be my deliverer and
get all the glory in the process!

Redeemed and Free

The Spirit of the Lord is upon me,
because he has anointed me
to proclaim good news to the poor.
He has sent me to proclaim liberty to the captives
and recovering of sight to the blind,
to set at liberty those who are oppressed,
to proclaim the year of the Lord's favor.

ISAIAH 61:1-2 ESV

When Jesus, the long awaited Messiah, revealed his deity to his family, his disciples, and the crowds, they were expecting a mighty king who would deliver them from their oppressors and establish his everlasting kingdom. What they got was a humble servant who dined with tax collectors and whose feet were cleansed by the tears of a prostitute. Jesus wasn't exactly what they thought he would be.

He was better! He came to bring salvation to those who were drowning in a sea of sin and sickness; those who were cast out and in need of holy redemption; those whom the religious leaders had deemed unworthy but whose hearts longed for true restoration. He came to redeem his people, but not in the way they expected.

Jesus, you delivered me from the bonds of sin and oppression through your death and resurrection. I praise you for my freedom! Holy Spirit, rest upon me and give me boldness to speak to others about this good news.

Refreshing Spring

"The water I give them," he said,
"becomes a perpetual spring within them,
watering them forever with eternal life."
JOHN 4:13-14 TLB

Have you ever been so thirsty you thought you'd never be able to take in enough water to quench your thirst? Maybe you've been somewhere so hot you were sure you would jump in a dirty puddle just to cool off. Imagine stumbling upon an oasis in the middle of the desert or a crystal clear swimming hole at the bottom of a waterfall in the jungle. How refreshing that would be!

The word *refreshment* itself sounds like a cool drink for the weary soul. God's Word is our source of life and energy. It gives us what we so desperately need, and it's available all the time! If you spend time in the Scriptures, you'll find his Word is in you, waiting to revitalize and invigorate you.

God, your Word will never run dry. Your water is life-giving and eternal—refreshing! A perpetual spring is in me ready to be drawn upon at any moment of the day or night. How encouraging this is to me when I am tired, frustrated, sad, and confused.

DAY 332

He Gives Me Rest

"So everyone, come to me! Are you weary, carrying a heavy burden? Then come to me. I will refresh your life, for I am your oasis. Simply join your life with mine. Learn my ways and you'll discover that I'm gentle, humble, easy to please. You will find refreshment and rest in me. For all that I require of you will be pleasant and easy to bear."

MATTHEW 11:28-30 TPT

There are times when grief leaves you bone tired. The thought of doing even the most simple task seems overwhelming. Getting out of bed, getting dressed, cooking dinner, or taking kids to practice become insurmountable chores. The world continues to spin, and you can think of nothing you'd like better than to stop and get off for a while. Trying to keep up with life's demands feels impossible. So don't try.

Admit your weakness and ask God for his strength. You will find that he is very resourceful when you allow him to be. Someone shows up on your doorstep with dinner? Accept it. That was a gift of rest from God. A friend swings by to pick up your kids for practice? Say thank you. That was God, too. Accepting that we need help can sometimes be the hardest part.

God, I am so grateful that you are gentle, humble, and easy to please.
Help me to find my rest and strength in you today.

All Things New

Bless the LORD, O my soul,
and forget not all his benefits,
who forgives all your iniquity,
who heals all your diseases,
who redeems your life from the pit,
who crowns you with steadfast love and mercy,
who satisfies you with good
so that your youth is renewed like the eagle's.

PSALM 103:2-5 ESV

Is it reasonable to believe that a marathon runner can finish a race without a single replenishing cup of water? Would it be fair to expect a doctor, after working a 36-hour shift, to have the energy to perform one last tedious surgery? Can a child be expected not to lick the spatula that mixed the cookie dough? Should a foreigner be familiar with the customs of a new land?

We know that humans have limits. We need to eat and drink regularly. We get tired and cranky if we don't have enough sleep. Our emotions can be overwhelmed by life's great upheavals. Whether you are at peak performance or running on empty, needing renewal now or in the future, God alone can give you what you need because he knows your limits and capabilities. He knows that you need time to refuel, space to recover your strength, and that sometimes a little cookie dough goes a long way.

God, I need your renewal. I know that I cannot be strong forever. I need you to replenish my energy, renew my mind, and give me strength.

Come Away

My beloved speaks and says to me:
"Arise, my love, my beautiful one, and come away,
for behold, the winter is past; the rain is over and gone.
The flowers appear on the earth, the time of
singing has come."

SONG OF SOLOMON 2:10-12 ESV

Some say that romance is dead. It's not for God: the lover of our souls. He desires nothing more than time with his creation! It can be a little uncomfortable to have his gaze so intently upon us though. We're nothing special, after all! Not beauty queens, academic scholars, or athletic prodigies of any kind. We might not be musical, or crafty, or organized. Our house might be a mess, and we could probably use a manicure.

Do you feel a bit squeamish under such an adoring gaze? There is good news for you! You are, in fact, his beautiful one! And he does, indeed, want to bring you out of the cold winter. He's finished the watering season and it is finally—*finally*—time to rejoice in the season of renewal.

Heavenly Father, I don't know why I feel uncomfortable under your gaze. You love me more than anyone else ever could! Regardless of how unworthy I think I am, I want to rise up and come away with you.

Weight of Worry

Anxiety in a man's heart weighs him down,
but a good word makes him glad.

PROVERBS 12:25 ESV

Worry fills our head with questions that may never have answers and possibilities that may never come to pass. We become wearied as even our momentary troubles outweigh our peace. It is in these times that the encouraging words of a friend can become the catalyst to change our uncertainty into strength and our doubt into restored faith.

By surrounding ourselves with the type of people who regularly speak the truth, we unknowingly secure our own peace and future gladness.

God, when I begin to feel anxious, I pray that you would bring a friend to speak your truth to me. Help me also to be an encouraging friend who brings peace to those around me.

Childlike Faith

*"I thank you, Father, Lord of heaven and earth,
that you have hidden these things from the wise
and understanding and revealed them to little children."*
MATTHEW 11:25 ESV

There are many things we can learn from our children. Jesus taught this
when the disciples were asking him who would be the greatest in the
kingdom of heaven. We don't know definitively why they were asking, but
we can make the assumption that they weren't at all expecting the answer
Jesus gave. He brought a child into their midst and said that unless they
became like a child, they would never enter the kingdom of heaven.

A child's faith in God knows no doubt. They believe—quite simply—that
he is who he says he is and he will do what he says he will do. They aren't
discouraged, and they have no reason to doubt his faithfulness. God
challenges us to have that kind of faith: sincere and pure.

*God, give me the kind of faith that doesn't give up.
In spite of discouragement, I want to trust you like a child would.*

Escape from Battle

No temptation has overtaken you except what is common to mankind. And God is faithful; he will not let you be tempted beyond what you can bear. But when you are tempted, he will also provide a way out so that you can endure it.

1 CORINTHIANS 10:13 NIV

Maybe you wrestle with anger or greed. Perhaps your struggle is with pride or vanity. It could be that you find it difficult to be honest or kind. Whatever your battle, you don't battle alone. We all have struggles, but God will not allow us to struggle with something too big to conquer.

We can be confident in every battle, in every struggle, and in every temptation, God will give us a way out. An escape plan is ready. When we face temptation, we can ask God for his help. He is faithful, and he will answer our cry.

God, help me with the battles I am facing today.
I know that you will rescue me and strengthen me.

The Offender's Heart

As those who have been chosen of God, holy and beloved, put on a heart of compassion, kindness, humility, gentleness and patience; bearing with one another, and forgiving each other, whoever has a complaint against anyone; just as the Lord forgave you, so also should you.

COLOSSIANS 3:12-13 NASB

When someone hurts us deeply, it isn't easy to look past the offense and into the offender's heart. But that is exactly what God does for us, and he wants us to do the same for others. More often than not, we will discover the offender drowning in their own sea of hurt and despair. They, too, need a great measure of love.

If we ask God to see our offenders the way he views them, we will develop a deep understanding and compassion for them. Our hurts may pale in comparison to their pain. We see that they are lost and desire someone to help them. We give them kindness and grace just as God gave it to us.

Father, help me show grace and compassion to those who have hurt me. Change my heart toward them. Let me see them the way you see them. Thank you for your kindness toward me.

DAY 339

A Pillar

The LORD is my rock and my fortress and my deliverer,
My God, my rock, in whom I take refuge;
My shield and the horn of my salvation, my stronghold.
PSALM 18:2 NASB

We never know how we will react when tragedy strikes, when we are beyond our understanding, or when we are faced with an unshakeable circumstance. What can we do to prepare ourselves? Not much in the physical world. But we can prune our hearts. We can ask for total dependence on our Father. We can more fully understand how deep and wide and long his love is for us, so that when we are faced with uncertainty, we cling to what we know is certain—Jesus.

Jesus is our ultimate support. He is our rock. He is our pillar of strength when we feel unsteady and uncertain. When we question, he is our answer. When we cry out for help, he is our comfort. When we ask why, he whispers his truth of a plan for our lives.

Lord, I need you. When circumstances are beyond my control,
I cling to you, my pillar of strength.

Integrity Is Possible

Let integrity and uprightness preserve me,
For I wait for You.
PSALM 25:21 NKJV

Having integrity means we lack nothing and live perfectly. It sounds impossible. But in Christ, we are made whole and complete—free from any blemish and stain. Therefore, integrity is present in every believer.

The good news is it's not something we have to search for or summon up. We are able to live in integrity and make choices according to his will because of the work that God has already done in us. Our integrity is compromised only when we choose to walk out of his wholeness.

God I realize that I can only act in integrity if I let you lead me. There is no perfection outside of you. Make me whole and complete as I wait on you.

Delete

To the praise of the glory of His grace, which He freely bestowed on us
in Him we have redemption through His blood,
the forgiveness of our trespasses, according to the riches
of His grace which He lavished on us.

EPHESIANS 1:6-8 NASB

Immediately after the moment, we want to hit delete. We want to go back in time just a few minutes when we could feel our blood pressure rising and knew we might say something we'd regret. We knew we might lose control because we just couldn't handle it anymore.

But the moment comes, we react, and then we apologize: it's the vicious cycle of our humanness. Thankfully, through the blood of Jesus Christ and our repentance, we are forgiven, set free, and released of the burden of our mistakes. We are given a clean slate to start over. And some days that gift feels bigger than other days. Some days, we rely heavily on the grace of our Lord and Savior just to get through the day. And that is okay.

God, there are so many times I want to hit "delete," or go back and change something I've said or done. Thank you that your gift of forgiveness is unlimited. I embrace that gift today.

DAY 342

The Voice of Love

"I have given them the glory you gave me, so they may be one as we are one. I am in them and you are in me. May they experience such perfect unity that the world will know that you sent me and that you love them as much as you love me."

JOHN 17:22-23 NLT

When we live for other voices, we will quickly become worn out and discouraged. Other people's expectations for how we should live, act, and be are sometimes unreachable. There is one voice that matters, and it can come in a variety of forms—the voice of God.

What God would tell us is that we are loved, we are cherished, and we add significant value. We are his beloved, his children, his beautiful creation. This is the voice that matters. This is the voice to come back to when we feel like we're not enough.

Father, help me to ignore the voices that don't matter.
Nothing changes the love you have for me.
Today, I choose to sit and soak in that love.

Transformation

I am certain that God, who began the good work within you, will continue
his work until it is finally finished on the day when Christ Jesus returns.

PHILIPPIANS 1:6 NLT

When we give our lives to God, we expect to be radically and completely
changed from the inside out. We get frustrated and discouraged when we
discover old habits are hard to break, and we keep getting ensnared in the
same temptation.

It is tempting to quit. But we should be encouraged! We are new in Christ;
his work in us is continual. Sanctification is a process—a very tough and
painful one. But his grace will cover us and he promises to complete his
work. He hasn't left us or abandoned us.

Lord, sometimes I'm so frustrated that I am not the person I want
to be. Thank you that you are transforming me through your Spirit
and by your Word. I look forward to your finished work in me.

Afraid of Monsters

I sought the LORD, and he answered me
and delivered me from all my fears.
Those who look to him are radiant,
and their faces shall never be ashamed.

PSALM 34:4-5 ESV

As children we were fearful of monsters under the bed, or we were frightened by the thought of what could be lurking in the dark corners of the room. As irrational as those fears were, they were real to us. We froze, dared not to breathe or cry out and shut our eyes tightly bidding sleep to come. The nights and the darkness they brought seemed endless.

As adults we still fear monsters; however, these days they take the form of an irate boss, difficulty with a relationship, an unfavorable medical diagnosis, or a credit card bill. Fear grips us in a real and powerful way, immobilizing us. If we aren't careful, fear can destroy our peace of mind. As a child of God, you can cry out to him, confident that he will help. You can shake fear and know that whatever monster you face, you don't face it alone.

God, the monsters in my life can be overwhelming. Thank you for the promise in your Word that tells me you will deliver me from all of my fears when I seek you. I ask you for peace today, and the radiance of a face that looks to you.

Transparency

Perfume and incense bring joy to the heart,
and the pleasantness of a friend
springs from their heartfelt advice.
PROVERBS 27:9 NIV

It is okay to cry over spilled milk. It really is. We all have hard days—days where we wake up late, we lose the keys, we can't find matching socks… and then the milk spills! We have those days where we just want to throw in the towel and call it quits. For some reason, we think we have to have it all together, all the time. We don't though. It is okay to be transparent with each other. By doing so we allow others to love us, encourage us, and pray for us.

Sharing our struggles not only lessens our burdens but reinforces the fact that we are not alone. It also gives permission for others to be transparent as well.

Father, I give up the idea that I need to have everything together. I need others in my life to help encourage me. Show me the friends I can be transparent with, and help me be a trustworthy friend to them as well.

Face of Kindness

"Come," my heart says, "seek his face!"
Your face, LORD, do I seek.
Do not hide your face from me.
PSALM 27:8-9 NRSV

Do you ever long to see God's face? Do you wonder what it looks like when he looks at you? Be assured, his eyes are more gentle than you expect. His expression is more tender than you thought, and his posture is more approachable than you perceived. This isn't just a cute idea. We know it is true because we know what he looked like when he walked the earth. We have direct accounts of how he responded to people with humble hearts. He welcomed them and gave them words that brought freedom.

We can picture the nicest person we know—the person who never seems to be bothered by anything and listens attentively to everyone. While that person might be noteworthy in their godliness, they are only a mere reflection of the kindness of God.

Father God, you are so consistent in your love for me.
You never have a bad day, and you don't look at me
with disgust when I do. Thank you for your face
that is tender and kind as it gazes on me.

Ancient Paths

"Stand at the crossroads and look;
ask for the ancient paths,
ask where the good way is, and walk in it,
and you will find rest for your souls."
JEREMIAH 6:16 NIV

It's fun to get something new—especially if you are a techy who loves gadgets. The long lines at Apple stores around the country prove that most of us are enamored with the latest and greatest. We don't like being outdated or not living on the cutting edge.

At times we can feel a bit outdated in our spiritual lives and need a refreshing touch from God. We may need reviving, but in the kingdom of God, old is better. In fact, ancient is best! In our church, worship styles change, programs and methods, too, but one thing must remain old, and that is the truth of God's Word. The old-time religion is still what rescues people from perishing. Since there is no need to update the gospel, perhaps what we need is just a fresh anointing of the Holy Spirit to fill us with contentment and rest for our souls.

Heavenly Father, I am in need today of a touch from you.
My spirit feels dry and outdated and my soul needs refreshment.
I want to follow your ancient paths where the good way is,
so give me a fresh beginning this day!

Inner Beauty

Don't be concerned about the outward beauty of fancy hairstyles, expensive jewelry, or beautiful clothes. You should clothe yourselves instead with the beauty that comes from within, the unfading beauty of a gentle and quiet spirit, which is so precious to God.

1 PETER 3:3-4 NLT

We all want to feel good about how we look, so we often spend time doing what we can to cover the weaknesses and enhance the strengths. We want to be beautiful. But God's definition of beauty is very different from the world's. Consider this story: God sent the prophet Samuel to Bethlehem to choose one of Jesse's sons to replace King Saul. When Samuel saw the oldest, Eliab, he thought, "Surely this is the one." That's when God charged Samuel not to look at the outward appearance because the Lord looks at the heart.

What is beautiful to God? We know he already loves what we look like—he created us! What is beautiful to him is a gentle and quiet spirit. As we adorn ourselves with love, graciousness, and kindness, we are living out true beauty that will draw others to Christ. Are you obsessing about your outward appearance? Remember, God is looking at your heart.

Lord, I have to admit that I fuss too much about how I look. I know as I become more like you, your beauty will be seen in me.

Brokenness

The LORD is close to the brokenhearted;
he rescues those whose spirits are crushed.
PSALM 34:18 NLT

Broken things are considered worthless and thrown away—the shattered glass, the old toy, the pen that has run out of ink. The world is full of people with hearts that are broken by betrayal, disappointment, or loss. At some point, all of our hearts were broken by sin, selfishness, pride, and willfulness: strongholds that God needed to break in our lives.

There is a beauty to brokenness because in the mending process we see Jesus at work. When we are broken, we are ripe for repair and need to turn to the master rebuilder. When we come to Christ with a repentant heart, God draws close to save us. When life gets tough and circumstances crush the spirit, God draws close to comfort us. When our desperation drives us to our knees, God draws close to deliver us. Is your heart broken today? Cry out to the master rebuilder. He will begin the work.

Lord, I need some repair work done in my heart today.
Thank you for being broken so my brokenness can be healed.

Choosing Contentment

Yet true godliness with contentment is itself great wealth.
After all, we brought nothing with us when we came into the world,
and we can't take anything with us when we leave it.
1 TIMOTHY 6:6-7 NLT

So many people in this world are motivated by the desire to have more. Perhaps we are tempted by the lure of materialism more than we care to admit. The temptation is hard to avoid as we are bombarded by the media at every turn. The rich man in Mark 10 had trouble with this issue. He was unable to give up his possessions and money to follow the Lord.

Most of us are not rich in the eyes of the world, but as Christians, when we come to a place of contentment with what God has given us, we are indeed rich. Godliness with contentment is itself great wealth. Are you struggling today with discontent or even covetousness? Surrender your desires to the Lord; choose contentment and enjoy what you have!

Dear Lord, I am so sorry I am discontented with what you have provided for me. I surrender my desires to you and thank you, because when I have you, I have everything I need.

Unusual Courage

When they saw the courage of Peter and John and realized that
they were unschooled, ordinary men, they were astonished
and they took note that these men had been with Jesus.

ACTS 4:13 NIV

Remember the cripple who sat daily at the temple gate to beg? Peter and
John came by, but they didn't give him any money. They healed him by
the powerful name of Jesus. This did not go unnoticed by the religious
leaders. The two apostles were called before the council where they faced
an intimidating group of men who had the authority to throw them in jail.
Fearlessly, Peter took the floor and leveled a powerful indictment against
them. They had crucified Jesus, whose power had healed the leper. The
council was appalled by the boldness of two ordinary, unschooled men. The
explanation for their courage? They had been with Jesus!

Is there a situation you are facing that calls for greater courage than you
can muster? Well, have you been with Jesus lately? You don't have to be
particularly gifted or educated to show unusual courage in a scary situation.
You have Jesus. He will give you exactly what you need.

Dear Lord, I need a large dose of courage today.
I pray that you would fill me with boldness
by the power of your Holy Spirit.

Freedom to Soar

It is for freedom that Christ has set us free.

GALATIANS 5:1 NIV

Freedom is a wonderful thing! We live in a free country where we can worship God, speak our minds, and enjoy unlimited opportunities without fear or restraint. Yet in spite of these liberties, we sometimes feel bound to the humdrum routine of daily life—somewhat like a hamster in its wheel. There seems to be no way of escaping the routine of joyless living.

This is not God's plan for us. Life naturally consists of responsibilities that can seem relentless, but we can simultaneously soar like the eagles in joyful freedom. Are you feeling trapped by routine today? Take a moment and fix your eyes on Jesus, soak in his presence, feel the spark of divine life that was ignited in you when you first surrendered your heart to him. Thank him for freedom from sin, fear, bondage, and hopelessness. It was for freedom that Christ set us free!

*Lord, thank you for the incredible gift of freedom
both in my country and in my soul! Help me face
my tasks today with joy, and set my spirit free.*

DAY 353

All Things

I can do all things through Him who strengthens me.
PHILIPPIANS 4:13 NASB

A young college student swallowed down panic each time she had to get up in public speaking class. On this particular day, hands sweaty, voice shaky, and knees knocking, she stood up to face her classmates for her five-minute speech. The professor was impressed by the presentation and asked her to give her message to the entire student body in the chapel service. Interestingly enough, the talk was on Philippians 4:13. How could she refuse in good conscience? On the appointed day, praying like crazy, and on the verge of a meltdown, she did the deed! God proved to be true to his Word and showed her in this small way that indeed, she could do a difficult thing because Jesus was her strength.

What are you facing this very day? Something completely out of your comfort zone? Something that evokes a creeping fear from the very core of your being and blankets you with dread? Be comforted in knowing that God will never ask you to do something that he will not enable you to do.

Oh Lord, how grateful I am that I don't have to try to be strong and courageous on my own. You are my source. Give me today what I need to carry out your will.

Home

*"I will live with them
and walk among them,
and I will be their God,
and they will be my people."*

2 CORINTHIANS 6:16 NIV

There's no place like home! Home is where we feel safe and secure; it's a place we can put our feet up, catch our breath, and unwind. We have our own set of keys, and we come and go with freedom. Home is where our heart is.

Perhaps home is not like that for you and you long for such a place. The great news is that our Father in heaven has already prepared one for you—not just in eternity, but also in the here and now. Remember, he is Emmanuel, the God who is walking and living among us. He gives us keys to his home where we can function with his authority, blessing, and power. Rushing to our Daddy with any need at any time, we can rest in the fact that whatever way he answers is the very best. We can relax, rest, and trust, knowing we are safe and secure in his presence. When we are with Jesus, we are home.

Oh Father, I want to live in such a place! My home here on earth needs some remodeling, but the home you've provided for me is perfectly designed to accommodate my heart. Thank you!

Hope

Why, my soul, are you downcast?
Why so disturbed within me?
Put your hope in God,
for I will yet praise him,
my Savior and my God.

PSALM 42:5 NIV

As a child you might recall a time when you longed to have a certain new toy and hoped with all your heart Santa would come through! You know the pain of disappointment if it wasn't under the tree and also the joy if it was! People everywhere are looking for someone or something to put their hope in while unaware that the greatest source of hope is found in Jesus Christ.

What are you hoping for today? Are you hoping a key person in your life or your circumstances will change? Fulfillment of such a hope cannot be guaranteed. However, when we place our hope in Christ, then every longing we have will be fulfilled! God knows what we really need, so he may have to tweak our longings a bit to fit his plans. But when our hope and trust are directed toward the God of all hope, we will not be disappointed.

Lord, conform the longings of my heart—all of my hopes—
to the mold you have fashioned for me. My hope is in you
and I will wait. I know that all of my desires are known
to you and you give me what I really need.

I Want to Know You

Oh, that we might know the LORD!
Let us press on to know him.
He will respond to us as surely as the arrival
of dawnor the coming of rains in early spring.

HOSEA 6:3 NLT

Hosea was a prophet with a most unusual assignment. He was led to marry a prostitute as a picture of Israel's unfaithfulness to God. In seeking to restore his own adulterous wife, Hosea demonstrated God's love and desire to restore his chosen people. The Israelites had turned to other gods, trusting in their own strength and military power rather than in the Lord. God allowed much tragedy to befall them in order to persuade them to return to him. Under these very heartbreaking circumstances, Hosea's impassioned plea reaches our ears today, "Let us press on to know him."

Have you been wayward lately—perhaps trusting in other people or in your own wisdom to solve your everyday problems? Have you made activities or busyness or even ministries your priority and relegated God to the back shelf? Oh, let us press on to know him! He will respond to us as surely as the arrival of dawn. As we seek him, he will reciprocate as surely as the coming of rains in early spring.

Lord, increase my desire to know you! I want to press on to greater knowledge of you, but life so often gets in the way. Today I resolve to seek you first.

The Eternal Gift

> "Give glory to God in heaven,
> and on earth let there be peace among the
> people who please God."
>
> LUKE 2:14 NCV

Christmas trees might be secular decorations, but they invoke, in Christians, thoughts of a more precious tree: the cross. Jesus came to us on Christmas day for the purpose of bringing peace to his people through the cross of Calvary.

Christ's mission was to redeem us from every thought, word, or action that didn't match up to our God-likeness. He destroyed our sins and silenced our enemy, permanently, on the cross. He empowered us for victory. Each of us carries his glory as a child of the Most High God. This is a Christmas gift for each of us to open every day.

Holy Father, thank you for this gift. Please toss out the broken ornaments of my life, and remake me according to your glory. Give me peace. I affirm you as my Lord, and I'll take orders from you. Thank you for loving me so tenderly. I love you, too.

Greatest Gift

> "For God did not send his Son into the world to condemn the world,
> but to save the world through him."
>
> JOHN 3:17 NIV

Have you ever considered what happened in heaven on the day earth received the greatest gift in the history of *forever*? When Jesus became a man, he set aside the indescribable power of being fully God and instead embraced humility and weakness. For a time, the Father lost the immeasurable depth of relationship with his Son and had to watch as Jesus learned obedience through suffering. There is truly no greater sacrifice than what both Father and Son made to declare to us all that we are loved.

Without the work of the Holy Spirit, the incarnation of Jesus would not have been possible. It is the same Spirit at work in you who reveals God's deep love and offers you the opportunity to receive his gift. Think on that as you celebrate the season of giving.

God, your gift to us is immeasurable, unfathomable,
and indescribable. I am humbled by your outpouring
of love to all of mankind despite our unworthiness.
Thank you.

Christmas Gift

"She will give birth to a son, and you are to give
him the name Jesus, because he will save his
people from their sins"

MATTHEW 1:21 NIV

The Christmas season is one of love. It is a season of remembering that the God of the universe came down to earth as a babe, changing everything. It is a season of longing with the adventure of Advent. It is a testament of celebration. Trees. Twinkling lights. Comfy jammies. Warm tea. Friends. Family. Traditions. Delicious food. Presents. Thoughtfulness. Comfort. Joy. Beauty. Salvation… in the form of a baby.

The Christmas season is about salvation. It is a beginning to be cherished and devoured at the same time. We recognize the gift of Jesus and what it meant for God to send him down to save us. He truly is the best gift of all.

God, in the busyness of this Christmas season,
I choose to stop and remember what it is all about.
I am saved because of your gift. Thank you.

My Christmas Song

"The Root of Jesse will spring up,
one who will arise to rule over the nations;
in him the Gentiles will hope."

ROMANS 15:12 NIV

Jesus, a Jew, came so all people would be qualified to experience his indescribable hope, joy, and peace as they placed their faith in him. It's not a wonder that a great band of angels joined together in praise that night. Jesus is the true basis for every believer's hope and joy, for this season and for all time.

You may be alone today or with many people. You may be reading this Christmas day, or you may be catching up after a flurry of activity. Perhaps you are flipping through this book, and you've stopped on this passage. Wherever you are, and whatever your circumstance, you have a gift from the Lord for this very day. It's okay; a Christmas gift from God doesn't expire! The gift God has for you, each and every day, is this: he is your strength and your song. And he always will be.

Jesus, thank you for being my Christmas song.
You are in touch with what I need to fill my soul,
even when I do not know. Thank you for your kindness in
coming to earth so I could become your child.
The thought of this fills my soul with gratitude.

Power to Transform

We are made right with God by placing our
faith in Jesus Christ. And this is true for everyone
who believes, no matter who we are.

ROMANS 3:22 NLT

God has the power to transform anything. We may think that a person or situation is completely beyond redemption—but God can reclaim even the most impossible of hearts and circumstances. We may have lost faith in believing for something, but God never does because he knows what he is capable of.

God, who has the power to speak the universe into existence, can certainly intervene in a situation and have his way in it. God, who commanded the dead to walk out of a tomb, can surely soften the heart of even the most hardened soul.

*Thank you, God, that you offer redemption for my heart,
my life, and my circumstances. Help me to trust you fully
in the redemptive process so that I can enjoy the benefit of a life
that has been changed by you.*

Taking Account

"Where your treasure is, there your heart will be also."
LUKE 12:34 NIV

A financial advisor would ask you to take account for every last dollar spent over the course of three months. The reason for this exercise is to clearly show our priorities. Where does our money go? Once we know, we can readjust our spending according to our overall financial plan.

The same method could be applied to general living. Where do we spend our time? If we tracked the time we invested into our relationships with loved ones, would we come up short? When we feel like our relationship with God is lacking, it is good to evaluate where we devote the majority of our time and focus. Do we seek him? Do we spend time in his Word?

God, I want to make you a priority in my life again.
Help me to show you and others where my treasure
and my heart really are.

Abundant Life

"I am the door; if anyone enters through Me, he will be saved, and will go in and out and find pasture. The thief comes only to steal and kill and destroy; I came that they may have life, and have it abundantly."

JOHN 10:9-10 NASB

Many have suffered the trauma of having a thief break into their home. Perhaps you have. As you know, a thief's design is entirely selfish—to obtain his own desires no matter the cost to others. In a spiritual sense, the thief (Satan) has a similar motive, only with a much darker objective. He not only wants to steal your joy, your faith, and your very life, he wants the destruction of your soul.

In contrast to that, we have the good shepherd. He came not to take away, but to give abundantly! His gifts go beyond forgiveness and salvation from sin. He desires that our lives be more than simple, bare existence, but rather abundant and satisfying, blessed all the way from the present through eternity. Take this truth into your day and live exuberantly!

Lord, help me recognize the attempts of the thief to rob me of my joy and faith. I thank you for being my good shepherd and showering my life with abundance.

Minimal

Remember that the Lord will reward
each one of us for the good we do.
EPHESIANS 6:8 NLT

A more simple life. A life with less clutter. A life with less to-dos. A life where less is more. A life of margin. A life, simply put, less busy. All of these we might desire for ourselves, and yet, we have a really hard time getting there. There is always a laundry list of responsibility not allowing much room for margin.

It is okay to be happy with a calm life. It is okay to *un-busy* your very busy life. It is most definitely okay to start using the word *no* more often. On the other end of this very busy life, we will find less stress, less anxiety, and less disappointment.

Jesus, my treasure is my relationship with you. It's not what I say or what I do. I know you desire my heart and I want to give it to you fully. Help me create a simpler life so I can hear your gentle whisper beckoning me to come.

Mourning into Dancing

May your unfailing love be my comfort,
according to your promise to your servant.

PSALM 119:76 NIV

Grief can look so different for each person, but it all fits into the same heart-wrenching mold of confusion, anger, sadness, and doubt. More often than not, grief surprises us with an upheaval of all we knew to be solid in life. Trusting in a God who loves us unconditionally gets muddled in those moments. Our solid foundation becomes spongy and uncertain.

Hopefully, with the gentle knocks on our hearts to remember his great love for us, the confusion turns into understanding and sadness into joy for the moments we were able to share. Our spongy, doubt-filled mind will cling to the truth that we knew deep in our souls—that God is good and he has a plan for our lives.

Lord God, there are times when I've doubted your plan for my life. Seasons of grief have made it hard to see that there will be laughter and peace once again. Help me trust in your promise of comfort in those moments.

Wisdom in Every Situation

Then you will understand what is right, just, and fair,
and you will find the right way to go.
For wisdom will enter your heart,
and knowledge will fill you with joy.
Wise choices will watch over you.
Understanding will keep you safe.

PROVERBS 2:9-11 NLT

All of life is a test. As we live each day, the tests we face teach us valuable lessons. It may seem backwards: usually lessons are learned to prepare us for a test. But in life, the test often comes first. Through the lessons, God gives us the wisdom we need for the next test.

It's a safe bet that the tests will keep coming. Thankfully, our hearts gain understanding every time. Tension and uncertainty melt away; joy blossoms. Solomon's advice is that we listen to wisdom, apply it, and learn as we go. Then we will have understanding; we will find the right path with wisdom in our hearts and joy from knowledge.

God, you have taught me so many valuable lessons
from life's tests. I take joy in the wisdom I have
gained from those tests. Thank you for giving me
the opportunity to make wise choices.